Police and Criminal Evidence Act 1984

Part V

Questioning and Treatment of Persons by Police

Section
53. Abolition of certain powers of constables to search persons.
54. Searches of detained persons.
55. Intimate searches.
56. Right to have someone informed when arrested.
57. Additional rights of children and young persons.
58. Access to legal advice.
59. Legal aid for persons at police stations.
60. Tape-recording of interviews.
61. Fingerprinting.
62. Intimate samples.
63. Other samples.
64. Destruction of fingerprints and samples.
65. Part V—supplementary.

Part VI

Codes of Practice—General

66. Codes of practice.
67. Codes of practice—supplementary.

Part VII

Documentary Evidence in Criminal Proceedings

68. Evidence from documentary records.
69. Evidence from computer records.
70. Provisions supplementary to sections 68 and 69.
71. Microfilm copies.
72. Part VII—supplementary.

Part VIII

Evidence in Criminal Proceedings—General

Convictions and acquittals

73. Proof of convictions and acquittals.
74. Conviction as evidence of commission of offence.
75. Provisions supplementary to section 74.

Confessions

Section
76. Confessions.
77. Confessions by mentally handicapped persons.
78. Exclusion of unfair evidence.

Miscellaneous

79. Time for taking accused's evidence.
80. Competence and compellability of accused's spouse.
81. Advance notice of expert evidence in Crown Court.

Part VIII—supplementary

82. Part VIII—interpretation.

PART IX

POLICE COMPLAINTS AND DISCIPLINE

The Police Complaints Authority

83. Establishment of the Police Complaints Authority.

Handling of complaints etc.

84. Preliminary.
85. Investigation of complaints: standard procedure.
86. Investigation of complaints against senior officers.
87. References of complaints to Authority.
88. References of other matters to Authority.
89. Supervision of investigations by Authority.
90. Steps to be taken after investigation—general.
91. Steps to be taken where accused has admitted charges.
92. Powers of Authority to direct reference of reports etc. to Director of Public Prosecutions.
93. Powers of Authority as to disciplinary charges.
94. Disciplinary tribunals.
95. Information as to the manner of dealing with complaints etc.
96. Constabularies maintained by authorities other than police authorities.
97. Reports.
98. Restriction on disclosure of information.
99. Regulations.
100. Regulations—supplementary.

Amendments of discipline provisions

101. Discipline regulations.
102. Representation at disciplinary proceedings.
103. Disciplinary appeals.

General

104. Restrictions on subsequent proceedings.
105. Guidelines concerning discipline, complaints etc.

Part X

Police—General

Section
106. Arrangements for obtaining the views of the community on policing.
107. Police officers performing duties of higher rank.
108. Deputy chief constables.
109. Amendments relating to Police Federations.
110. Functions of special constables in Scotland.
111. Regulations for Police Forces and Police Cadets—Scotland.
112. Metropolitan police officers.

Part XI

Miscellaneous and Supplementary

113. Application of Act to Armed Forces.
114. Application of Act to Customs and Excise.
115. Expenses.
116. Meaning of " serious arrestable offence ".
117. Power of constable to use reasonable force.
118. General interpretation.
119. Amendments and repeals.
120. Extent.
121. Commencement.
122. Short title.

Schedules:

Schedule 1—Special procedure.

Schedule 2—Preserved powers of arrest.

Schedule 3—Provisions supplementary to sections 68 and 69.
    Part I—Provisions supplementary to section 68.
    Part II—Provisions supplementary to section 69.
    Part III—Provisions supplementary to sections 68 and 69.

Schedule 4—The Police Complaints Authority.
    Part I—General.
    Part II—Transitional.

Schedule 5—Serious arrestable offences.
    Part I—Offences mentioned in section 116(2)(*a*).
    Part II—Offences mentioned in section 116(2)(*b*).

Schedule 6—Minor and consequential amendments.
- Part I—England and Wales.
- Part II—Other amendments.

Schedule 7—Repeals.
- Part I—Enactments repealed in consequence of Parts I to V.
- Part II—Enactments repealed in relation to criminal proceedings in consequence of Part VII.
- Part III—Enactments repealed generally in consequence of Part VII.
- Part IV—Enactments repealed in relation to criminal proceedings in consequence of Part VIII.
- Part V—Enactments repealed generally in consequence of Part VIII.
- Part VI—Miscellaneous repeals.

ELIZABETH II

Police and Criminal Evidence Act 1984

1984 CHAPTER 60

An Act to make further provision in relation to the powers and duties of the police, persons in police detention, criminal evidence, police discipline and complaints against the police; to provide for arrangements for obtaining the views of the community on policing and for a rank of deputy chief constable; to amend the law relating to the Police Federations and Police Forces and Police Cadets in Scotland; and for connected purposes. [31st October 1984]

BE IT ENACTED by the Queen's most Excellent Majesty, by and with the advice and consent of the Lords Spiritual and Temporal, and Commons, in this present Parliament assembled, and by the authority of the same, as follows:—

PART I

POWERS TO STOP AND SEARCH

1.—(1) A constable may exercise any power conferred by this section— *Power of constable to stop and search persons, vehicles etc.*

    (a) in any place to which at the time when he proposes to exercise the power the public or any section of the public has access, on payment or otherwise, as of right or by virtue of express or implied permission; or

    (b) in any other place to which people have ready access at the time when he proposes to exercise the power but which is not a dwelling.

(2) Subject to subsection (3) to (5) below, a constable—
- (a) may search—
  - (i) any person or vehicle;
  - (ii) anything which is in or on a vehicle,
  for stolen or prohibited articles; and
- (b) may detain a person or vehicle for the purpose of such a search.

(3) This section does not give a constable power to search a person or vehicle or anything in or on a vehicle unless he has reasonable grounds for suspecting that he will find stolen or prohibited articles.

(4) If a person is in a garden or yard occupied with and used for the purposes of a dwelling or on other land so occupied and used, a constable may not search him in the exercise of the power conferred by this section unless the constable has reasonable grounds for believing—
- (a) that he does not reside in the dwelling; and
- (b) that he is not in the place in question with the express or implied permission of a person who resides in the dwelling.

(5) If a vehicle is in a garden or yard occupied with and used for the purposes of a dwelling or on other land so occupied and used, a constable may not search the vehicle or anything in or on it in the exercise of the power conferred by this section unless he has reasonable grounds for believing—
- (a) that the person in charge of the vehicle does not reside in the dwelling; and
- (b) that the vehicle is not in the place in question with the express or implied permission of a person who resides in the dwelling.

(6) If in the course of such a search a constable discovers an article which he has reasonable grounds for suspecting to be a stolen or prohibited article, he may seize it.

(7) An article is prohibited for the purposes of this Part of this Act if it is—
- (a) an offensive weapon; or
- (b) an article—
  - (i) made or adapted for use in the course of or in connection with an offence to which this sub-paragraph applies; or
  - (ii) intended by the person having it with him for such use by him or by some other person.

(8) The offences to which subsection (7)(b)(i) above applies are—

(a) burglary;

(b) theft;

(c) offences under section 12 of the Theft Act 1968 (taking motor vehicle or other conveyance without authority); and

(d) offences under section 15 of that Act (obtaining property by deception).

(9) In this Part of this Act " offensive weapon " means any article—

(a) made or adapted for use for causing injury to persons; or

(b) intended by the person having it with him for such use by him or by some other person.

2.—(1) A constable who detains a person or vehicle in the exercise—

(a) of the power conferred by section 1 above; or

(b) of any other power—

(i) to search a person without first arresting him; or

(ii) to search a vehicle without making an arrest,

need not conduct a search if it appears to him subsequently—

(i) that no search is required; or

(ii) that a search is impracticable.

(2) If a constable contemplates a search, other than a search of an unattended vehicle, in the exercise—

(a) of the power conferred by section 1 above; or

(b) of any other power, except the power conferred by section 6 below and the power conferred by section 27(2) of the Aviation Security Act 1982—

(i) to search a person without first arresting him; or

(ii) to search a vehicle without making an arrest,

it shall be his duty, subject to subsection (4) below, to take reasonable steps before he commences the search to bring to the attention of the appropriate person—

(i) if the constable is not in uniform, documentary evidence that he is a constable; and

(ii) whether he is in uniform or not, the matters specified in subsection (3) below;

and the constable shall not commence the search until he has performed that duty.

(3) The matters referred to in subsection (2)(ii) above are—
- (a) the constable's name and the name of the police station to which he is attached;
- (b) the object of the proposed search;
- (c) the constable's grounds for proposing to make it; and
- (d) the effect of section 3(7) or (8) below, as may be appropriate.

(4) A constable need not bring the effect of section 3(7) or (8) below to the attention of the appropriate person if it appears to the constable that it will not be practicable to make the record in section 3(1) below.

(5) In this section " the appropriate person " means—
- (a) if the constable proposes to search a person, that person; and
- (b) if he proposes to search a vehicle, or anything in or on a vehicle, the person in charge of the vehicle.

(6) On completing a search of an unattended vehicle or anything in or on such a vehicle in the exercise of any such power as is mentioned in subsection (2) above a constable shall leave a notice—
- (a) stating that he has searched it;
- (b) giving the name of the police station to which he is attached;
- (c) stating that an application for compensation for any damage caused by the search may be made to that police station; and
- (d) stating the effect of section 3(8) below.

(7) The constable shall leave the notice inside the vehicle unless it is not reasonably practicable to do so without damaging the vehicle.

(8) The time for which a person or vehicle may be detained for the purposes of such a search is such time as is reasonably required to permit a search to be carried out either at the place where the person or vehicle was first detained or nearby.

(9) Neither the power conferred by section 1 above nor any other power to detain and search a person without first arresting him or to detain and search a vehicle without making an arrest is to be construed—
- (a) as authorising a constable to require a person to remove any of his clothing in public other than an outer coat, jacket or gloves; or
- (b) as authorising a constable not in uniform to stop a vehicle.

(10) This section and section 1 above apply to vessels, aircraft and hovercraft as they apply to vehicles.

3.—(1) Where a constable has carried out a search in the exercise of any such power as is mentioned in section 2(1) above, other than a search—

(a) under section 6 below; or

(b) under section 27(2) of the Aviation Security Act 1982,

he shall make a record of it in writing unless it is not practicable to do so.

Duty to make records concerning searches.

1982 c. 36.

(2) If—

(a) a constable is required by subsection (1) above to make a record of a search; but

(b) it is not practicable to make the record on the spot,

he shall make it as soon as practicable after the completion of the search.

(3) The record of a search of a person shall include a note of his name, if the constable knows it, but a constable may not detain a person to find out his name.

(4) If a constable does not know the name of a person whom he has searched, the record of the search shall include a note otherwise describing that person.

(5) The record of a search of a vehicle shall include a note describing the vehicle.

(6) The record of a search of a person or a vehicle—

(a) shall state—

(i) the object of the search;

(ii) the grounds for making it;

(iii) the date and time when it was made;

(iv) the place where it was made;

(v) whether anything, and if so what, was found;

(vi) whether any, and if so what, injury to a person or damage to property appears to the constable to have resulted from the search; and

(b) shall identify the constable making it.

(7) If a constable who conducted a search of a person made a record of it, the person who was searched shall be entitled to a copy of the record if he asks for one before the end of the period specified in subsection (9) below.

(8) If—

(a) the owner of a vehicle which has been searched or the person who was in charge of the vehicle at the time

PART I

when it was searched asks for a copy of the record of the search before the end of the period specified in subsection (9) below ; and

(b) the constable who conducted the search made a record of it,

the person who made the request shall be entitled to a copy.

(9) The period mentioned in subsections (7) and (8) above is the period of 12 months beginning with the date on which the search was made.

(10) The requirements imposed by this section with regard to records of searches of vehicles shall apply also to records of searches of vessels, aircraft and hovercraft.

Road checks.

4.—(1) This section shall have effect in relation to the conduct of road checks by police officers for the purpose of ascertaining whether a vehicle is carrying—

(a) a person who has committed an offence other than a road traffic offence or a vehicles excise offence ;

(b) a person who is a witness to such an offence ;

(c) a person intending to commit such an offence ; or

(d) a person who is unlawfully at large.

1972 c. 20.

(2) For the purposes of this section a road check consists of the exercise in a locality of the power conferred by section 159 of the Road Traffic Act 1972 in such a way as to stop during the period for which its exercise in that way in that locality continues all vehicles or vehicles selected by any criterion.

(3) Subject to subsection (5) below, there may only be such a road check if a police officer of the rank of superintendent or above authorises it in writing.

(4) An officer may only authorise a road check under subsection (3) above—

(a) for the purpose specified in subsection (1)(a) above, if he has reasonable grounds—

(i) for believing that the offence is a serious arrestable offence ; and

(ii) for suspecting that the person is, or is about to be, in the locality in which vehicles would be stopped if the road check were authorised ;

(b) for the purpose specified in subsection (1)(b) above, if he has reasonable grounds for believing that the offence is a serious arrestable offence ;

(c) for the purpose specified in subsection (1)(c) above, if he has reasonable grounds—

(i) for believing that the offence would be a serious arrestable offence ; and

(ii) for suspecting that the person is, or is about to be, in the locality in which vehicles would be stopped if the road check were authorised;

(d) for the purpose specified in subsection (1)(d) above, if he has reasonable grounds for suspecting that the person is, or is about to be, in that locality.

(5) An officer below the rank of superintendent may authorise such a road check if it appears to him that it is required as a matter of urgency for one of the purposes specified in subsection (1) above.

(6) If an authorisation is given under subsection (5) above, it shall be the duty of the officer who gives it—

(a) to make a written record of the time at which he gives it; and

(b) to cause an officer of the rank of superintendent or above to be informed that it has been given.

(7) The duties imposed by subsection (6) above shall be performed as soon as it is practicable to do so.

(8) An officer to whom a report is made under subsection (6) above may, in writing, authorise the road check to continue.

(9) If such an officer considers that the road check should not continue, he shall record in writing—

(a) the fact that it took place; and

(b) the purpose for which it took place.

(10) An officer giving an authorisation under this section shall specify the locality in which vehicles are to be stopped.

(11) An officer giving an authorisation under this section, other than an authorisation under subsection (5) above—

(a) shall specify a period, not exceeding seven days, during which the road check may continue; and

(b) may direct that the road check—

(i) shall be continuous; or

(ii) shall be conducted at specified times,

during that period.

(12) If it appears to an officer of the rank of superintendent or above that a road check ought to continue beyond the period for which it has been authorised he may, from time to time, in writing specify a further period, not exceeding seven days, during which it may continue.

PART I

(13) Every written authorisation shall specify—
  (a) the name of the officer giving it;
  (b) the purpose of the road check; and
  (c) the locality in which vehicles are to be stopped.

(14) The duties to specify the purposes of a road check imposed by subsections (9) and (13) above include duties to specify any relevant serious arrestable offence.

(15) Where a vehicle is stopped in a road check, the person in charge of the vehicle at the time when it is stopped shall be entitled to obtain a written statement of the purpose of the road check if he applies for such a statement not later than the end of the period of twelve months from the day on which the vehicle was stopped.

(16) Nothing in this section affects the exercise by police officers of any power to stop vehicles for purposes other than those specified in subsection (1) above.

Reports of recorded searches and of road checks.
1964 c. 48

5.—(1) Every annual report—
  (a) under section 12 of the Police Act 1964; or
  (b) made by the Commissioner of Police of the Metropolis,
shall contain information—
    (i) about searches recorded under section 3 above which have been carried out in the area to which the report relates during the period to which it relates; and
    (ii) about road checks authorised in that area during that period under section 4 above.

(2) The information about searches shall not include information about specific searches but shall include—
  (a) the total numbers of searches in each month during the period to which the report relates—
      (i) for stolen articles;
      (ii) for offensive weapons; and
      (iii) for other prohibited articles;
  (b) the total number of persons arrested in each such month in consequence of searches of each of the descriptions specified in paragraph (a)(i) to (iii) above.

(3) The information about road checks shall include information—
  (a) about the reason for authorising each road check; and
  (b) about the result of each of them.

6.—(1) A constable employed by statutory undertakers may stop, detain and search any vehicle before it leaves a goods area included in the premises of the statutory undertakers.

Statutory undertakers etc.

(2) In this section "goods area" means any area used wholly or mainly for the storage or handling of goods.

(3) For the purposes of section 6 of the Public Stores Act 1875, any person appointed under the Special Constables Act 1923 to be a special constable within any premises which are in the possession or under the control of British Nuclear Fuels Limited shall be deemed to be a constable deputed by a public department and any goods and chattels belonging to or in the possession of British Nuclear Fuels Limited shall be deemed to be Her Majesty's Stores.

1875 c. 25.
1923 c. 11.

(4) In the application of subsection (3) above to Northern Ireland, for the reference to the Special Constables Act 1923 there shall be substituted a reference to paragraph 1(2) of Schedule 2 to the Emergency Laws (Miscellaneous Provisions) Act 1947.

1947 c. 10.
(11 & 12 Geo. 6.)

7.—(1) The following enactments shall cease to have effect—
  (a) section 8 of the Vagrancy Act 1824;
  (b) section 66 of the Metropolitan Police Act 1839;
  (c) section 11 of the Canals (Offences) Act 1840;
  (d) section 19 of the Pedlars Act 1871;
  (e) section 33 of the County of Merseyside Act 1980; and
  (f) section 42 of the West Midlands County Council Act 1980.

Part I— supplementary.
1824 c. 83.
1839 c. 47.
1840 c. 50.
1871 c. 96.
1980 c. x.
1980 c. xi.

(2) There shall also cease to have effect—
  (a) so much of any enactment contained in an Act passed before 1974, other than—
    (i) an enactment contained in a public general Act; or
    (ii) an enactment relating to statutory undertakers,
  as confers power on a constable to search for stolen or unlawfully obtained goods; and
  (b) so much of any enactment relating to statutory undertakers as provides that such a power shall not be exercisable after the end of a specified period.

(3) In this Part of this Act "statutory undertakers" means persons authorised by any enactment to carry on any railway, light railway, road transport, water transport, canal, inland navigation, dock or harbour undertaking.

Part II

Powers of Entry, Search and Seizure

Search warrants

Power of justice of the peace to authorise entry and search of premises.

8.—(1) If on an application made by a constable a justice of the peace is satisfied that there are reasonable grounds for believing—

(a) that a serious arrestable offence has been committed; and

(b) that there is material on premises specified in the application which is likely to be of substantial value (whether by itself or together with other material) to the investigation of the offence; and

(c) that the material is likely to be relevant evidence; and

(d) that it does not consist of or include items subject to legal privilege, excluded material or special procedure material; and

(e) that any of the conditions specified in subsection (3) below applies,

he may issue a warrant authorising a constable to enter and search the premises.

(2) A constable may seize and retain anything for which a search has been authorised under subsection (1) above.

(3) The conditions mentioned in subsection (1)(e) above are—

(a) that it is not practicable to communicate with any person entitled to grant entry to the premises;

(b) that it is practicable to communicate with a person entitled to grant entry to the premises but it is not practicable to communicate with any person entitled to grant access to the evidence;

(c) that entry to the premises will not be granted unless a warrant is produced;

(d) that the purpose of a search may be frustrated or seriously prejudiced unless a constable arriving at the premises can secure immediate entry to them.

(4) In this Act " relevant evidence ", in relation to an offence, means anything that would be admissible in evidence at a trial for the offence.

(5) The power to issue a warrant conferred by this section is in addition to any such power otherwise conferred.

Special provisions as to access.

9.—(1) A constable may obtain access to excluded material or special procedure material for the purposes of a criminal investigation by making an application under Schedule 1 below and in accordance with that Schedule.

(2) Any Act (including a local Act) passed before this Act under which a search of premises for the purposes of a criminal investigation could be authorised by the issue of a warrant to a constable shall cease to have effect so far as it relates to the authorisation of searches—

    (a) for items subject to legal privilege; or

    (b) for excluded material; or

    (c) for special procedure material consisting of documents or records other than documents.

10.—(1) Subject to subsection (2) below, in this Act "items subject to legal privilege" means—

    (a) communications between a professional legal adviser and his client or any person representing his client made in connection with the giving of legal advice to the client;

    (b) communications between a professional legal adviser and his client or any person representing his client or between such an adviser or his client or any such representative and any other person made in connection with or in contemplation of legal proceedings and for the purposes of such proceedings; and

    (c) items enclosed with or referred to in such communications and made—

        (i) in connection with the giving of legal advice; or

        (ii) in connection with or in contemplation of legal proceedings and for the purposes of such proceedings,

when they are in the possession of a person who is entitled to possession of them.

(2) Items held with the intention of furthering a criminal purpose are not items subject to legal privilege.

11.—(1) Subject to the following provisions of this section, in this Act "excluded material" means—

    (a) personal records which a person has acquired or created in the course of any trade, business, profession or other occupation or for the purposes of any paid or unpaid office and which he holds in confidence;

    (b) human tissue or tissue fluid which has been taken for the purposes of diagnosis or medical treatment and which a person holds in confidence;

(c) journalistic material which a person holds in confidence and which consists—

(i) of documents ; or

(ii) of records other than documents.

(2) A person holds material other than journalistic material in confidence for the purposes of this section if he holds it subject—

(a) to an express or implied undertaking to hold it in confidence ; or

(b) to a restriction on disclosure or an obligation of secrecy contained in any enactment, including an enactment contained in an Act passed after this Act.

(3) A person holds journalistic material in confidence for the purposes of this section if—

(a) he holds it subject to such an undertaking, restriction or obligation ; and

(b) it has been continuously held (by one or more persons) subject to such an undertaking, restriction or obligation since it was first acquired or created for the purposes of journalism.

Meaning of "personal records".

12. In this Part of this Act " personal records " means documentary and other records concerning an individual (whether living or dead) who can be identified from them and relating—

(a) to his physical or mental health ;

(b) to spiritual counselling or assistance given or to be given to him ; or

(c) to counselling or assistance given or to be given to him, for the purposes of his personal welfare, by any voluntary organisation or by any individual who—

(i) by reason of his office or occupation has responsibilities for his personal welfare ; or

(ii) by reason of an order of a court has responsibilities for his supervision.

Meaning of "journalistic material".

13.—(1) Subject to subsection (2) below, in this Act " journalistic material " means material acquired or created for the purposes of journalism.

(2) Material is only journalistic material for the purposes of this Act if it is in the possession of a person who acquired or created it for the purposes of journalism.

(3) A person who receives material from someone who intends that the recipient shall use it for the purposes of journalism is to be taken to have acquired it for those purposes.

PART II

Meaning of "special procedure material".

14.—(1) In this Act "special procedure material" means—
    (a) material to which subsection (2) below applies; and
    (b) journalistic material, other than excluded material.

(2) Subject to the following provisions of this section, this subsection applies to material, other than items subject to legal privilege and excluded material, in the possession of a person who—
    (a) acquired or created it in the course of any trade, business, profession or other occupation or for the purpose of any paid or unpaid office; and
    (b) holds it subject—
        (i) to an express or implied undertaking to hold it in confidence; or
        (ii) to a restriction or obligation such as is mentioned in section 11(2)(b) above.

(3) Where material is acquired—
    (a) by an employee from his employer and in the course of his employment; or
    (b) by a company from an associated company,
it is only special procedure material if it was special procedure material immediately before the acquisition.

(4) Where material is created by an employee in the course of his employment, it is only special procedure material if it would have been special procedure material had his employer created it.

(5) Where material is created by a company on behalf of an associated company, it is only special procedure material if it would have been special procedure material had the associated company created it.

(6) A company is to be treated as another's associated company for the purposes of this section if it would be so treated under section 302 of the Income and Corporation Taxes Act 1970.

1970 c. 10.

Search warrants—safeguards.

15.—(1) This section and section 16 below have effect in relation to the issue to constables under any enactment, including an enactment contained in an Act passed after this Act, of warrants to enter and search premises; and an entry on or search of premises under a warrant is unlawful unless it complies with this section and section 16 below.

(2) Where a constable applies for any such warrant, it shall be his duty—

PART II

(a) to state—
(i) the ground on which he makes the application; and
(ii) the enactment under which the warrant would be issued;
(b) to specify the premises which it is desired to enter and search; and
(c) to identify, so far as is practicable, the articles or persons to be sought.

(3) An application for such a warrant shall be made ex parte and supported by an information in writing.

(4) The constable shall answer on oath any question that the justice of the peace or judge hearing the application asks him.

(5) A warrant shall authorise an entry on one occasion only.

(6) A warrant—
(a) shall specify—
(i) the name of the person who applies for it;
(ii) the date on which it is issued;
(iii) the enactment under which it is issued; and
(iv) the premises to be searched; and
(b) shall identify, so far as is practicable, the articles or persons to be sought.

(7) Two copies shall be made of a warrant.

(8) The copies shall be clearly certified as copies.

Execution of warrants.

16.—(1) A warrant to enter and search premises may be executed by any constable.

(2) Such a warrant may authorise persons to accompany any constable who is executing it.

(3) Entry and search under a warrant must be within one month from the date of its issue.

(4) Entry and search under a warrant must be at a reasonable hour unless it appears to the constable executing it that the purpose of a search may be frustrated on an entry at a reasonable hour.

(5) Where the occupier of premises which are to be entered and searched is present at the time when a constable seeks to execute a warrant to enter and search them, the constable—
(a) shall identify himself to the occupier and, if not in uniform, shall produce to him documentary evidence that he is a constable;
(b) shall produce the warrant to him; and
(c) shall supply him with a copy of it.

(6) Where—
  (a) the occupier of such premises is not present at the time when a constable seeks to execute such a warrant; but
  (b) some other person who appears to the constable to be in charge of the premises is present,

subsection (5) above shall have effect as if any reference to the occupier were a reference to that other person.

(7) If there is no person present who appears to the constable to be in charge of the premises, he shall leave a copy of the warrant in a prominent place on the premises.

(8) A search under a warrant may only be a search to the extent required for the purpose for which the warrant was issued.

(9) A constable executing a warrant shall make an endorsement on it stating—
  (a) whether the articles or persons sought were found; and
  (b) whether any articles were seized, other than articles which were sought.

(10) A warrant which—
  (a) has been executed; or
  (b) has not been executed within the time authorised for its execution,

shall be returned—
  (i) if it was issued by a justice of the peace, to the clerk to the justices for the petty sessions area for which he acts; and
  (ii) if it was issued by a judge, to the appropriate officer of the court from which he issued it.

(11) A warrant which is returned under subsection (10) above shall be retained for 12 months from its return—
  (a) by the clerk to the justices, if it was returned under paragraph (i) of that subsection; and
  (b) by the appropriate officer, if it was returned under paragraph (ii).

(12) If during the period for which a warrant is to be retained the occupier of the premises to which it relates asks to inspect it, he shall be allowed to do so.

Entry and search without search warrant

17.—(1) Subject to the following provisions of this section, and without prejudice to any other enactment, a constable may enter and search any premises for the purpose—
  (a) of executing—
    (i) a warrant of arrest issued in connection with or arising out of criminal proceedings; or

PART II
1980 c. 43.

(ii) a warrant of commitment issued under section 76 of the Magistrates' Courts Act 1980;

(b) of arresting a person for an arrestable offence;

(c) of arresting a person for an offence under—

(i) section 1 (prohibition of uniforms in connection with political objects), 4 (prohibition of offensive weapons at public meetings and processions) or 5 (prohibition of offensive conduct conducive to breaches of the peace) of the Public Order Act 1936;

1936 c. 6

(ii) any enactment contained in sections 6 to 8 or 10 of the Criminal Law Act 1977 (offences relating to entering and remaining on property);

1977 c 45.

(d) of recapturing a person who is unlawfully at large and whom he is pursuing; or

(e) of saving life or limb or preventing serious damage to property.

(2) Except for the purpose specified in paragraph (e) of subsection (1) above, the powers of entry and search conferred by this section—

(a) are only exercisable if the constable has reasonable grounds for believing that the person whom he is seeking is on the premises; and

(b) are limited, in relation to premises consisting of two or more separate dwellings, to powers to enter and search—

(i) any parts of the premises which the occupiers of any dwelling comprised in the premises use in common with the occupiers of any other such dwelling; and

(ii) any such dwelling in which the constable has reasonable grounds for believing that the person whom he is seeking may be.

(3) The powers of entry and search conferred by this section are only exercisable for the purposes specified in subsection (1)(c)(ii) above by a constable in uniform.

(4) The power of search conferred by this section is only a power to search to the extent that is reasonably required for the purpose for which the power of entry is exercised.

(5) Subject to subsection (6) below, all the rules of common law under which a constable has power to enter premises without a warrant are hereby abolished.

(6) Nothing in subsection (5) above affects any power of entry to deal with or prevent a breach of the peace.

18.—(1) Subject to the following provisions of this section, a constable may enter and search any premises occupied or controlled by a person who is under arrest for an arrestable offence, if he has reasonable grounds for suspecting that there is on the premises evidence, other than items subject to legal privilege, that relates—

PART II
Entry and search after arrest.

(a) to that offence; or

(b) to some other arrestable offence which is connected with or similar to that offence.

(2) A constable may seize and retain anything for which he may search under subsection (1) above.

(3) The power to search conferred by subsection (1) above is only a power to search to the extent that is reasonably required for the purpose of discovering such evidence.

(4) Subject to subsection (5) below, the powers conferred by this section may not be exercised unless an officer of the rank of inspector or above has authorised them in writing.

(5) A constable may conduct a search under subsection (1) above—

(a) before taking the person to a police station; and

(b) without obtaining an authorisation under subsection (4) above,

if the presence of that person at a place other than a police station is necessary for the effective investigation of the offence.

(6) If a constable conducts a search by virtue of subsection (5) above, he shall inform an officer of the rank of inspector or above that he has made the search as soon as practicable after he has made it.

(7) An officer who—

(a) authorises a search; or

(b) is informed of a search under subsection (6) above,

shall make a record in writing—

(i) of the grounds for the search; and

(ii) of the nature of the evidence that was sought.

(8) If the person who was in occupation or control of the premises at the time of the search is in police detention at the time the record is to be made, the officer shall make the record as part of his custody record.

PART II
General power of seizure etc.

Seizure etc.

19.—(1) The powers conferred by subsections (2), (3) and (4) below are exercisable by a constable who is lawfully on any premises.

(2) The constable may seize anything which is on the premises if he has reasonable grounds for believing—

(*a*) that it has been obtained in consequence of the commission of an offence ; and

(*b*) that it is necessary to seize it in order to prevent it being concealed, lost, damaged, altered or destroyed.

(3) The constable may seize anything which is on the premises if he has reasonable grounds for believing—

(*a*) that it is evidence in relation to an offence which he is investigating or any other offence ; and

(*b*) that it is necessary to seize it in order to prevent the evidence being concealed, lost, altered or destroyed.

(4) The constable may require any information which is contained in a computer and is accessible from the premises to be produced in a form in which it can be taken away and in which it is visible and legible if he has reasonable grounds for believing—

(*a*) that—

(i) it is evidence in relation to an offence which he is investigating or any other offence ; or

(ii) it has been obtained in consequence of the commission of an offence ; and

(*b*) that it is necessary to do so in order to prevent it being concealed, lost, tampered with or destroyed.

(5) The powers conferred by this section are in addition to any power otherwise conferred.

(6) No power of seizure conferred on a constable under any enactment (including an enactment contained in an Act passed after this Act) is to be taken to authorise the seizure of an item which the constable exercising the power has reasonable grounds for believing to be subject to legal privilege.

PART II

Extension of powers of seizure to computerised information.

20.—(1) Every power of seizure which is conferred by an enactment to which this section applies on a constable who has entered premises in the exercise of a power conferred by an enactment shall be construed as including a power to require any information contained in a computer and accessible from the premises to be produced in a form in which it can be taken away and in which it is visible and legible.

(2) This section applies—

(a) to any enactment contained in an Act passed before this Act;

(b) to sections 8 and 18 above;

(c) to paragraph 13 of Schedule 1 to this Act; and

(d) to any enactment contained in an Act passed after this Act.

Access and copying.

21.—(1) A constable who seizes anything in the exercise of a power conferred by any enactment, including an enactment contained in an Act passed after this Act, shall, if so requested by a person showing himself—

(a) to be the occupier of premises on which it was seized; or

(b) to have had custody or control of it immediately before the seizure,

provide that person with a record of what he seized.

(2) The officer shall provide the record within a reasonable time from the making of the request for it.

(3) Subject to subsection (8) below, if a request for permission to be granted access to anything which—

(a) has been seized by a constable; and

(b) is retained by the police for the purpose of investigating an offence,

is made to the officer in charge of the investigation by a person who had custody or control of the thing immediately before it was so seized or by someone acting on behalf of such a person, the officer shall allow the person who made the request access to it under the supervision of a constable.

(4) Subject to subsection (8) below, if a request for a photograph or copy of any such thing is made to the officer in charge of the investigation by a person who had custody or control of the thing immediately before it was so seized, or by someone acting on behalf of such a person, the officer shall—

(a) allow the person who made the request access to it under the supervision of a constable for the purpose of photographing or copying it; or

PART II

(b) photograph or copy it, or cause it to be photographed or copied.

(5) A constable may also photograph or copy, or have photographed or copied, anything which he has power to seize, without a request being made under subsection (4) above.

(6) Where anything is photographed or copied under subsection (4)(b) above, the photograph or copy shall be supplied to the person who made the request.

(7) The photograph or copy shall be so supplied within a reasonable time from the making of the request.

(8) There is no duty under this section to grant access to, or to supply a photograph or copy of, anything if the officer in charge of the investigation for the purposes of which it was seized has reasonable grounds for believing that to do so would prejudice—

(a) that investigation;
(b) the investigation of an offence other than the offence for the purposes of investigating which the thing was seized; or
(c) any criminal proceedings which may be brought as a result of–
   (i) the investigation of which he is in charge; or
   (ii) any such investigation as is mentioned in paragraph (b) above.

Retention.

22.—(1) Subject to subsection (4) below, anything which has been seized by a constable or taken away by a constable following a requirement made by virtue of section 19 or 20 above may be retained so long as is necessary in all the circumstances.

(2) Without prejudice to the generality of subsection (1) above—

(a) anything seized for the purposes of a criminal investigation may be retained, except as provided by subsection (4) below—
   (i) for use as evidence at a trial for an offence; or
   (ii) for forensic examination or for investigation in connection with an offence; and
(b) anything may be retained in order to establish its lawful owner, where there are reasonable grounds for believing that it has been obtained in consequence of the commission of an offence.

(3) Nothing seized on the ground that it may be used—

(a) to cause physical injury to any person;

(b) to damage property;

(c) to interfere with evidence; or

(d) to assist in escape from police detention or lawful custody,

may be retained when the person from whom it was seized is no longer in police detention or the custody of a court or is in the custody of a court but has been released on bail.

(4) Nothing may be retained for either of the purposes mentioned in subsection (2)(a) above if a photograph or copy would be sufficient for that purpose.

(5) Nothing in this section affects any power of a court to make an order under section 1 of the Police (Property) Act 1897.

Supplementary

23. In this Act—

" premises " includes any place and, in particular, includes—

(a) any vehicle, vessel, aircraft or hovercraft;

(b) any offshore installation; and

(c) any tent or movable structure; and

" offshore installation " has the meaning given to it by section 1 of the Mineral Workings (Offshore Installations) Act 1971.

Part III

Arrest

24.—(1) The powers of summary arrest conferred by the following subsections shall apply—

(a) to offences for which the sentence is fixed by law;

(b) to offences for which a person of 21 years of age or over (not previously convicted) may be sentenced to imprisonment for a term of five years (or might be so sentenced but for the restrictions imposed by section 33 of the Magistrates' Courts Act 1980); and

(c) to the offences to which subsection (2) below applies,

and in this Act " arrestable offence " means any such offence.

(2) The offences to which this subsection applies are—

(a) offences for which a person may be arrested under the customs and excise Acts, as defined in section 1(1) of the Customs and Excise Management Act 1979;

(b) offences under the Official Secrets Acts 1911 and 1920 that are not arrestable offences by virtue of the term of imprisonment for which a person may be sentenced in respect of them;

(c) offences under section 14 (indecent assault on a woman), 22 (causing prostitution of women) or 23 (procuration of girl under 21) of the Sexual Offences Act 1956;

(d) offences under section 12(1) (taking motor vehicle or other conveyance without authority etc.) or 25(1) (going equipped for stealing, etc.) of the Theft Act 1968; and

(e) offences under section 1 of the Public Bodies Corrupt Practices Act 1889 (corruption in office) or section 1 of the Prevention of Corruption Act 1906 (corrupt transactions with agents).

(3) Without prejudice to section 2 of the Criminal Attempts Act 1981, the powers of summary arrest conferred by the following subsections shall also apply to the offences of—

(a) conspiring to commit any of the offences mentioned in subsection (2) above;

(b) attempting to commit any such offence;

(c) inciting, aiding, abetting, counselling or procuring the commission of any such offence;

and such offences are also arrestable offences for the purposes of this Act.

(4) Any person may arrest without a warrant—

(a) anyone who is in the act of committing an arrestable offence;

(b) anyone whom he has reasonable grounds for suspecting to be committing such an offence.

(5) Where an arrestable offence has been committed, any person may arrest without a warrant—

(a) anyone who is guilty of the offence;

(b) anyone whom he has reasonable grounds for suspecting to be guilty of it.

(6) Where a constable has reasonable grounds for suspecting that an arrestable offence has been committed, he may arrest without a warrant anyone whom he has reasonable grounds for suspecting to be guilty of the offence.

(7) A constable may arrest without a warrant—
  (a) anyone who is about to commit an arrestable offence;
  (b) anyone whom he has reasonable grounds for suspecting to be about to commit an arrestable offence.

25.—(1) Where a constable has reasonable grounds for suspecting that any offence which is not an arrestable offence has been committed or attempted, or is being committed or attempted, he may arrest the relevant person if it appears to him that service of a summons is impracticable or inappropriate because any of the general arrest conditions is satisfied.

General arrest conditions.

(2) In this section " the relevant person " means any person whom the constable has reasonable grounds to suspect of having committed or having attempted to commit the offence or of being in the course of committing or attempting to commit it.

(3) The general arrest conditions are—
  (a) that the name of the relevant person is unknown to, and cannot be readily ascertained by, the constable;
  (b) that the constable has reasonable grounds for doubting whether a name furnished by the relevant person as his name is his real name;
  (c) that—
      (i) the relevant person has failed to furnish a satisfactory address for service; or
      (ii) the constable has reasonable grounds for doubting whether an address furnished by the relevant person is a satisfactory address for service;
  (d) that the constable has reasonable grounds for believing that arrest is necessary to prevent the relevant person—
      (i) causing physical injury to himself or any other person;
      (ii) suffering physical injury;
      (iii) causing loss of or damage to property;
      (iv) committing an offence against public decency; or
      (v) causing an unlawful obstruction of the highway;
  (e) that the constable has reasonable grounds for believing that arrest is necessary to protect a child or other vulnerable person from the relevant person.

(4) For the purposes of subsection (3) above an address is a satisfactory address for service if it appears to the constable—
  (a) that the relevant person will be at it for a sufficiently long period for it to be possible to serve him with a summons; or

PART III

(*b*) that some other person specified by the relevant person will accept service of a summons for the relevant person at it.

(5) Nothing in subsection (3)(*d*) above authorises the arrest of a person under sub-paragraph (iv) of that paragraph except where members of the public going about their normal business cannot reasonably be expected to avoid the person to be arrested.

(6) This section shall not prejudice any power of arrest conferred apart from this section.

Repeal of statutory powers of arrest without warrant or order.

26.—(1) Subject to subsection (2) below, so much of any Act (including a local Act) passed before this Act as enables a constable—

(*a*) to arrest a person for an offence without a warrant; or
(*b*) to arrest a person otherwise than for an offence without a warrant or an order of a court,

shall cease to have effect.

(2) Nothing in subsection (1) above affects the enactments specified in Schedule 2 to this Act.

Fingerprinting of certain offenders.

27.—(1) If a person—

(*a*) has been convicted of a recordable offence;
(*b*) has not at any time been in police detention for the offence; and
(*c*) has not had his fingerprints taken—
 (i) in the course of the investigation of the offence by the police; or
 (ii) since the conviction,

any constable may at any time not later than one month after the date of the conviction require him to attend a police station in order that his fingerprints may be taken.

(2) A requirement under subsection (1) above—

(*a*) shall give the person a period of at least 7 days within which he must so attend; and
(*b*) may direct him to so attend at a specified time of day or between specified times of day.

(3) Any constable may arrest without warrant a person who has failed to comply with a requirement under subsection (1) above.

(4) The Secretary of State may by regulations make provision for recording in national police records convictions for such offences as are specified in the regulations.

(5) Regulations under this section shall be made by statutory instrument and shall be subject to annulment in pursuance of a resolution of either House of Parliament.

28.—(1) Subject to subsection (5) below, where a person is arrested, otherwise than by being informed that he is under arrest, the arrest is not lawful unless the person arrested is informed that he is under arrest as soon as is practicable after his arrest.

Information to be given on arrest.

(2) Where a person is arrested by a constable, subsection (1) above applies regardless of whether the fact of the arrest is obvious.

(3) Subject to subsection (5) below, no arrest is lawful unless the person arrested is informed of the ground for the arrest at the time of, or as soon as is practicable after, the arrest.

(4) Where a person is arrested by a constable, subsection (3) above applies regardless of whether the ground for the arrest is obvious.

(5) Nothing in this section is to be taken to require a person to be informed—

(a) that he is under arrest; or

(b) of the ground for the arrest,

if it was not reasonably practicable for him to be so informed by reason of his having escaped from arrest before the information could be given.

29. Where for the purpose of assisting with an investigation a person attends voluntarily at a police station or at any other place where a constable is present or accompanies a constable to a police station or any such other place without having been arrested—

Voluntary attendance at police station etc.

(a) he shall be entitled to leave at will unless he is placed under arrest;

(b) he shall be informed at once that he is under arrest if a decision is taken by a constable to prevent him from leaving at will.

30.—(1) Subject to the following provisions of this section, where a person—

Arrest elsewhere than at police station.

(a) is arrested by a constable for an offence; or

(b) is taken into custody by a constable after being arrested for an offence by a person other than a constable,

at any place other than a police station, he shall be taken to a police station by a constable as soon as practicable after the arrest.

(2) Subject to subsections (3) and (5) below, the police station to which an arrested person is taken under subsection (1) above shall be a designated police station.

PART III

(3) A constable to whom this subsection applies may take an arrested person to any police station unless it appears to the constable that it may be necessary to keep the arrested person in police detention for more than six hours.

(4) Subsection (3) above applies—
    (*a*) to a constable who is working in a locality covered by a police station which is not a designated police station ; and
    (*b*) to a constable belonging to a body of constables maintained by an authority other than a police authority.

(5) Any constable may take an arrested person to any police station if—
    (*a*) either of the following conditions is satisfied—
        (i) the constable has arrested him without the assistance of any other constable and no other constable is available to assist him ;
        (ii) the constable has taken him into custody from a person other than a constable without the assistance of any other constable and no other constable is available to assist him ; and
    (*b*) it appears to the constable that he will be unable to take the arrested person to a designated police station without the arrested person injuring himself, the constable or some other person.

(6) If the first police station to which an arrested person is taken after his arrest is not a designated police station, he shall be taken to a designated police station not more than six hours after his arrival at the first police station unless he is released previously.

(7) A person arrested by a constable at a place other than a police station shall be released if a constable is satisfied, before the person arrested reaches a police station, that there are no grounds for keeping him under arrest.

(8) A constable who releases a person under subsection (7) above shall record the fact that he has done so.

(9) The constable shall make the record as soon as is practicable after the release.

(10) Nothing in subsection (1) above shall prevent a constable delaying taking a person who has been arrested to a police station if the presence of that person elsewhere is necessary in order to carry out such investigations as it is reasonable to carry out immediately.

(11) Where there is delay in taking a person who has been arrested to a police station after his arrest, the reasons for the delay shall be recorded when he first arrives at a police station.

(12) Nothing in subsection (1) above shall be taken to affect—
- (a) paragraphs 16(3) or 18(1) of Schedule 2 to the Immigration Act 1971;
- (b) section 34(1) of the Criminal Justice Act 1972; or
- (c) paragraph 5 of Schedule 3 to the Prevention of Terrorism (Temporary Provisions) Act 1984 or any provision contained in an order under section 13 of that Act which authorises the detention of persons on board a ship or aircraft.

1971 c. 77.

1972 c. 71.

1984 c. 8.

(13) Nothing in subsection (10) above shall be taken to affect paragraph 18(3) of Schedule 2 to the Immigration Act 1971.

31. Where—
- (a) a person—
  - (i) has been arrested for an offence; and
  - (ii) is at a police station in consequence of that arrest; and
- (b) it appears to a constable that, if he were released from that arrest, he would be liable to arrest for some other offence,

he shall be arrested for that other offence.

Arrest for further offence.

32.—(1) A constable may search an arrested person, in any case where the person to be searched has been arrested at a place other than a police station, if the constable has reasonable grounds for believing that the arrested person may present a danger to himself or others.

Search upon arrest.

(2) Subject to subsections (3) to (5) below, a constable shall also have power in any such case—
- (a) to search the arrested person for anything—
  - (i) which he might use to assist him to escape from lawful custody; or
  - (ii) which might be evidence relating to an offence; and
- (b) to enter and search any premises in which he was when arrested or immediately before he was arrested for evidence relating to the offence for which he has been arrested.

(3) The power to search conferred by subsection (2) above is only a power to search to the extent that is reasonably required

PART III for the purpose of discovering any such thing or any such evidence.

(4) The powers conferred by this section to search a person are not to be construed as authorising a constable to require a person to remove any of his clothing in public other than an outer coat, jacket or gloves.

(5) A constable may not search a person in the exercise of the power conferred by subsection (2)(*a*) above unless he has reasonable grounds for believing that the person to be searched may have concealed on him anything for which a search is permitted under that paragraph.

(6) A constable may not search premises in the exercise of the power conferred by subsection (2)(*b*) above unless he has reasonable grounds for believing that there is evidence for which a search is permitted under that paragraph on the premises.

(7) In so far as the power of search conferred by subsection (2)(*b*) above relates to premises consisting of two or more separate dwellings, it is limited to a power to search—

(*a*) any dwelling in which the arrest took place or in which the person arrested was immediately before his arrest; and

(*b*) any parts of the premises which the occupier of any such dwelling uses in common with the occupiers of any other dwellings comprised in the premises.

(8) A constable searching a person in the exercise of the power conferred by subsection (1) above may seize and retain anything he finds, if he has reasonable grounds for believing that the person searched might use it to cause physical injury to himself or to any other person.

(9) A constable searching a person in the exercise of the power conferred by subsection (2)(*a*) above may seize and retain anything he finds, other than an item subject to legal privilege, if he has reasonable grounds for believing—

(a) that he might use it to assist him to escape from lawful custody; or

(b) that it is evidence of an offence or has been obtained in consequence of the commission of an offence.

(10) Nothing in this section shall be taken to affect the power conferred by paragraph 6 of Schedule 3 to the Prevention of Terrorism (Temporary Provisions) Act 1984.

1984 c. 8.

Execution of warrant not in possession of constable.
1980 c. 43.

33. In section 125 of the Magistrates' Courts Act 1980—

(*a*) in subsection (3), for the words " arrest a person charged with an offence " there shall be substituted the words " which this subsection applies ";

(b) the following subsection shall be added after that subsection—

" (4) The warrants to which subsection (3) above applies are—

(a) a warrant to arrest a person in connection with an offence;

(b) without prejudice to paragraph (a) above, a warrant under section 186(3) of the Army Act 1955, section 186(3) of the Air Force Act 1955, section 105(3) of the Naval Discipline Act 1957 or Schedule 5 to the Reserve Forces Act 1980 (desertion etc.);

1955 c. 18.
1955 c. 19.
1957 c. 53.
1980 c. 9.

(c) a warrant under—

(i) section 102 or 104 of the General Rate Act 1967 (insufficiency of distress);

1967 c. 9.

(ii) section 18(4) of the Domestic Proceedings and Magistrates' Courts Act 1978 (protection of parties to marriage and children of family); and

1978 c. 22.

(iii) section 55, 76, 93 or 97 above.".

Part IV

Detention

Detention—conditions and duration

34.—(1) A person arrested for an offence shall not be kept in police detention except in accordance with the provisions of this Part of this Act.

Limitations on police detention.

(2) Subject to subsection (3) below, if at any time a custody officer—

(a) becomes aware, in relation to any person in police detention, that the grounds for the detention of that person have ceased to apply; and

(b) is not aware of any other grounds on which the continued detention of that person could be justified under the provisions of this Part of this Act,

it shall be the duty of the custody officer, subject to subsection (4) below, to order his immediate release from custody.

(3) No person in police detention shall be released except on the authority of a custody officer at the police station where his detention was authorised or, if it was authorised at more than one station, a custody officer at the station where it was last authorised.

PART IV

(4) A person who appears to the custody officer to have been unlawfully at large when he was arrested is not to be released under subsection (2) above.

(5) A person whose release is ordered under subsection (2) above shall be released without bail unless it appears to the custody officer—

  (a) that there is need for further investigation of any matter in connection with which he was detained at any time during the period of his detention; or

  (b) that proceedings may be taken against him in respect of any such matter,

and, if it so appears, he shall be released on bail.

1972 c. 20.

(6) For the purposes of this Part of this Act a person arrested under section 7(5) of the Road Traffic Act 1972 is arrested for an offence.

Designated police stations.

35.—(1) The chief officer of police for each police area shall designate the police stations in his area which, subject to section 30(3) and (5) above, are to be the stations in that area to be used for the purpose of detaining arrested persons.

(2) A chief officer's duty under subsection (1) above is to designate police stations appearing to him to provide enough accommodation for that purpose.

1978 c. 30.

(3) Without prejudice to section 12 of the Interpretation Act 1978 (continuity of duties) a chief officer—

  (a) may designate a station which was not previously designated; and

  (b) may direct that a designation of a station previously made shall cease to operate.

(4) In this Act "designated police station" means a police station for the time being designated under this section.

Custody officers at police stations.

36.—(1) One or more custody officers shall be appointed for each designated police station.

(2) A custody officer for a designated police station shall be appointed—

  (a) by the chief officer of police for the area in which the designated police station is situated; or

  (b) by such other police officer as the chief officer of police for that area may direct.

(3) No officer may be appointed a custody officer unless he is of at least the rank of sergeant.

(4) An officer of any rank may perform the functions of a custody officer at a designated police station if a custody officer is not readily available to perform them.

(5) Subject to the following provisions of this section and to section 39(2) below, none of the functions of a custody officer in relation to a person shall be performed by an officer who at the time when the function falls to be performed is involved in the investigation of an offence for which that person is in police detention at that time.

(6) Nothing in subsection (5) above is to be taken to prevent a custody officer—

    (a) performing any function assigned to custody officers—

        (i) by this Act ; or

        (ii) by a code of practice issued under this Act ;

    (b) carrying out the duty imposed on custody officers by section 39 below ;

    (c) doing anything in connection with the identification of a suspect ; or

    (d) doing anything under section 8 of the Road Traffic Act 1972.

[1972 c. 20.]

(7) Where an arrested person is taken to a police station which is not a designated police station, the functions in relation to him which at a designated police station would be the functions of a custody officer shall be performed—

    (a) by an officer who is not involved in the investigation of an offence for which he is in police detention, if such an officer is readily available ; and

    (b) if no such officer is readily available, by the officer who took him to the station or any other officer.

(8) References to a custody officer in the following provisions of this Act include references to an officer other than a custody officer who is performing the functions of a custody officer by virtue of subsection (4) or (7) above.

(9) Where by virtue of subsection (7) above an officer of a force maintained by a police authority who took an arrested person to a police station is to perform the functions of a custody officer in relation to him, the officer shall inform an officer who—

    (a) is attached to a designated police station ; and

    (b) is of at least the rank of inspector,

that he is to do so.

(10) The duty imposed by subsection (9) above shall be performed as soon as it is practicable to perform it.

PART IV
Duties of custody officer before charge.

37.—(1) Where—
- (a) a person is arrested for an offence—
  - (i) without a warrant; or
  - (ii) under a warrant not endorsed for bail, or
- (b) a person returns to a police station to answer to bail,

the custody officer at each police station where he is detained after his arrest shall determine whether he has before him sufficient evidence to charge that person with the offence for which he was arrested and may detain him at the police station for such period as is necessary to enable him to do so.

(2) If the custody officer determines that he does not have such evidence before him, the person arrested shall be released either on bail or without bail, unless the custody officer has reasonable grounds for believing that his detention without being charged is necessary to secure or preserve evidence relating to an offence for which he is under arrest or to obtain such evidence by questioning him.

(3) If the custody officer has reasonable grounds for so believing, he may authorise the person arrested to be kept in police detention.

(4) Where a custody officer authorises a person who has not been charged to be kept in police detention, he shall, as soon as is practicable, make a written record of the grounds for the detention.

(5) Subject to subsection (6) below, the written record shall be made in the presence of the person arrested who shall at that time be informed by the custody officer of the grounds for his detention.

(6) Subsection (5) above shall not apply where the person arrested is, at the time when the written record is made—
- (a) incapable of understanding what is said to him;
- (b) violent or likely to become violent; or
- (c) in urgent need of medical attention.

(7) Subject to section 41(7) below, if the custody officer determines that he has before him sufficient evidence to charge the person arrested with the offence for which he was arrested, the person arrested—
- (a) shall be charged; or
- (b) shall be released without charge, either on bail or without bail.

(8) Where—
- (a) a person is released under subsection (7)(b) above; and

(b) at the time of his release a decision whether he should be prosecuted for the offence for which he was arrested has not been taken,

it shall be the duty of the custody officer so to inform him.

(9) If the person arrested is not in a fit state to be dealt with under subsection (7) above, he may be kept in police detention until he is.

(10) The duty imposed on the custody officer under subsection (1) above shall be carried out by him as soon as practicable after the person arrested arrives at the police station or, in the case of a person arrested at the police station, as soon as practicable after the arrest.

(11) Where—
- (a) an arrested juvenile who was arrested without a warrant is not released under subsection (2) above; and
- (b) it appears to the custody officer that a decision falls to be taken in pursuance of section 5(2) of the Children and Young Persons Act 1969 whether to lay an information in respect of an offence alleged to have been committed by the arrested juvenile,

it shall be the duty of the custody officer to inform him that such a decision falls to be taken and to specify the offence.

(12) It shall also be the duty of the custody officer—
- (a) to take such steps as are practicable to ascertain the identity of a person responsible for the welfare of the arrested juvenile; and
- (b) if—
    (i) he ascertains the identity of any such person; and
    (ii) it is practicable to give that person the information which subsection (11) above requires the custody officer to give to the arrested juvenile,
  to give that person the information as soon as it is practicable to do so.

(13) For the purposes of subsection (12) above the persons who may be responsible for the welfare of an arrested juvenile are—
- (a) his parent or guardian; and
- (b) any other person who has for the time being assumed responsibility for his welfare.

(14) If it appears to the custody officer that a supervision order, as defined in section 11 of the Children and Young Persons Act 1969, is in force in respect of the arrested juvenile,

PART IV

the custody officer shall also give the information to the person responsible for the arrested juvenile's supervision, as soon as it is practicable to do so.

(15) In this Part of this Act—

"arrested juvenile" means a person arrested with or without a warrant who appears to be under the age of 17 and is not excluded from this Part of this Act by section 52 below;

1980 c. 43.

"endorsed for bail" means endorsed with a direction for bail in accordance with section 117(2) of the Magistrates' Courts Act 1980.

Duties of custody officer after charge.

38.—(1) Where a person arrested for an offence otherwise than under a warrant endorsed for bail is charged with an offence, the custody officer shall order his release from police detention, either on bail or without bail, unless—

(a) if the person arrested is not an arrested juvenile—

(i) his name or address cannot be ascertained or the custody officer has reasonable grounds for doubting whether a name or address furnished by him as his name or address is his real name or address;

(ii) the custody officer has reasonable grounds for believing that the detention of the person arrested is necessary for his own protection or to prevent him from causing physical injury to any other person or from causing loss of or damage to property; or

(iii) the custody officer has reasonable grounds for believing that the person arrested will fail to appear in court to answer to bail or that his detention is necessary to prevent him from interfering with the administration of justice or with the investigation of offences or of a particular offence;

(b) if he is an arrested juvenile—

(i) any of the requirements of paragraph (a) above is satisfied; or

(ii) the custody officer has reasonable grounds for believing that he ought to be detained in his own interests.

(2) If the release of a person arrested is not required by subsection (1) above, the custody officer may authorise him to be kept in police detention.

(3) Where a custody officer authorises a person who has been charged to be kept in police detention, he shall, as soon as practicable, make a written record of the grounds for the detention.

PART IV

(4) Subject to subsection (5) below, the written record shall be made in the presence of the person charged who shall at that time be informed by the custody officer of the grounds for his detention.

(5) Subsection (4) above shall not apply where the person charged is, at the time when the written record is made—

(a) incapable of understanding what is said to him;

(b) violent or likely to become violent; or

(c) in urgent need of medical attention.

(6) Where a custody officer authorises an arrested juvenile to be kept in police detention under subsection (1) above, the custody officer shall, unless he certifies that it is impracticable to do so, make arrangements for the arrested juvenile to be taken into the care of a local authority and detained by the authority; and it shall be lawful to detain him in pursuance of the arrangements.

(7) A certificate made under subsection (6) above in respect of an arrested juvenile shall be produced to the court before which he is first brought thereafter.

(8) In this Part of this Act "local authority" has the same meaning as in the Children and Young Persons Act 1969.

1969 c.54.

Responsibilities in relation to persons detained.

39.—(1) Subject to subsections (2) and (4) below, it shall be the duty of the custody officer at a police station to ensure—

(a) that all persons in police detention at that station are treated in accordance with this Act and any code of practice issued under it and relating to the treatment of persons in police detention; and

(b) that all matters relating to such persons which are required by this Act or by such codes of practice to be recorded are recorded in the custody records relating to such persons.

(2) If the custody officer, in accordance with any code of practice issued under this Act, transfers or permits the transfer of a person in police detention—

(a) to the custody of a police officer investigating an offence for which that person is in police detention; or

(b) to the custody of an officer who has charge of that person outside the police station,

the custody officer shall cease in relation to that person to be subject to the duty imposed on him by subsection (1)(a) above; and it shall be the duty of the officer to whom the transfer is made to ensure that he is treated in accordance with the provi-

PART IV sions of this Act and of any such codes of practice as are mentioned in subsection (1) above.

(3) If the person detained is subsequently returned to the custody of the custody officer, it shall be the duty of the officer investigating the offence to report to the custody officer as to the manner in which this section and the codes of practice have been complied with while that person was in his custody.

(4) If an arrested juvenile is transferred to the care of a local authority in pursuance of arrangements made under section 38(6) above, the custody officer shall cease in relation to that person to be subject to the duty imposed on him by subsection (1) above.

(5) It shall be the duty of a local authority to make available to an arrested juvenile who is in the authority's care in pursuance of such arrangements such advice and assistance as may be appropriate in the circumstances.

(6) Where—
 (a) an officer of higher rank than the custody officer gives directions relating to a person in police detention; and
 (b) the directions are at variance—
  (i) with any decision made or action taken by the custody officer in the performance of a duty imposed on him under this Part of this Act; or
  (ii) with any decision or action which would but for the directions have been made or taken by him in the performance of such a duty,

the custody officer shall refer the matter at once to an officer of the rank of superintendent or above who is responsible for the police station for which the custody officer is acting as custody officer.

Review of police detention.

40.—(1) Reviews of the detention of each person in police detention in connection with the investigation of an offence shall be carried out periodically in accordance with the following provisions of this section—
 (a) in the case of a person who has been arrested and charged, by the custody officer; and
 (b) in the case of a person who has been arrested but not charged, by an officer of at least the rank of inspector who has not been directly involved in the investigation.

(2) The officer to whom it falls to carry out a review is referred to in this section as a " review officer ".

(3) Subject to subsection (4) below—
- (*a*) the first review shall be not later than six hours after the detention was first authorised;
- (*b*) the second review shall be not later than nine hours after the first;
- (*c*) subsequent reviews shall be at intervals of not more than nine hours.

(4) A review may be postponed—
- (*a*) if, having regard to all the circumstances prevailing at the latest time for it specified in subsection (3) above, it is not practicable to carry out the review at that time;
- (*b*) without prejudice to the generality of paragraph (*a*) above—
  - (i) if at that time the person in detention is being questioned by a police officer and the review officer is satisfied that an interruption of the questioning for the purpose of carrying out the review would prejudice the investigation in connection with which he is being questioned; or
  - (ii) if at that time no review officer is readily available.

(5) If a review is postponed under subsection (4) above it shall be carried out as soon as practicable after the latest time specified for it in subsection (3) above.

(6) If a review is carried out after postponement under subsection (4) above, the fact that it was so carried out shall not affect any requirement of this section as to the time at which any subsequent review is to be carried out.

(7) The review officer shall record the reasons for any postponement of a review in the custody record.

(8) Subject to subsection (9) below, where the person whose detention is under review has not been charged before the time of the review, section 37(1) to (6) above shall have effect in relation to him, but with the substitution—
- (*a*) of references to the person whose detention is under review for references to the person arrested; and
- (*b*) of references to the review officer for references to the custody officer.

(9) Where a person has been kept in police detention by virtue of section 37(9) above, section 37(1) to (6) shall not have effect in relation to him but it shall be the duty of the review officer to determine whether he is yet in a fit state.

PART IV

(10) Where the person whose detention is under review has been charged before the time of the review, section 38(1) to (6) above shall have effect in relation to him, but with the substitution of references to the person whose detention is under review for references to the person arrested.

(11) Where—

(a) an officer of higher rank than the review officer gives directions relating to a person in police detention; and

(b) the directions are at variance—

(i) with any decision made or action taken by the review officer in the performance of a duty imposed on him under this Part of this Act; or

(ii) with any decision or action which would but for the directions have been made or taken by him in the performance of such a duty,

the review officer shall refer the matter at once to an officer of the rank of superintendent or above who is responsible for the police station for which the review officer is acting as review officer in connection with the detention.

(12) Before determining whether to authorise a person's continued detention the review officer shall give—

(a) that person (unless he is asleep); or

(b) any solicitor representing him who is available at the time of the review,

an opportunity to make representations to him about the detention.

(13) Subject to subsection (14) below, the person whose detention is under review or his solicitor may make representations under subsection (12) above either orally or in writing.

(14) The review officer may refuse to hear oral representations from the person whose detention is under review if he considers that he is unfit to make such representations by reason of his condition or behaviour.

Limits on period of detention without charge.

41.—(1) Subject to the following provisions of this section and to sections 42 and 43 below, a person shall not be kept in police detention for more than 24 hours without being charged.

(2) The time from which the period of detention of a person is to be calculated (in this Act referred to as "the relevant time")—

(a) in the case of a person to whom this paragraph applies, shall be—

(i) the time at which that person arrives at the relevant police station; or

(ii) the time 24 hours after the time of that person's arrest,

whichever is the earlier;

(b) in the case of a person arrested outside England and Wales, shall be—

(i) the time at which that person arrives at the first police station to which he is taken in the police area in England or Wales in which the offence for which he was arrested is being investigated; or

(ii) the time 24 hours after the time of that person's entry into England and Wales,

whichever is the earlier;

(c) in the case of a person who—

(i) attends voluntarily at a police station; or

(ii) accompanies a constable to a police station without having been arrested,

and is arrested at the police station, the time of his arrest;

(d) in any other case, except where subsection (5) below applies, shall be the time at which the person arrested arrives at the first police station to which he is taken after his arrest.

(3) Subsection (2)(a) above applies to a person if—

(a) his arrest is sought in one police area in England and Wales;

(b) he is arrested in another police area; and

(c) he is not questioned in the area in which he is arrested in order to obtain evidence in relation to an offence for which he is arrested;

and in sub-paragraph (i) of that paragraph "the relevant police station" means the first police station to which he is taken in the police area in which his arrest was sought.

(4) Subsection (2) above shall have effect in relation to a person arrested under section 31 above as if every reference in it to his arrest or his being arrested were a reference to his arrest or his being arrested for the offence for which he was originally arrested.

(5) If—

(a) a person is in police detention in a police area in England and Wales (" the first area "); and

(b) his arrest for an offence is sought in some other police area in England and Wales (" the second area "); and

PART IV

      (c) he is taken to the second area for the purposes of investigating that offence, without being questioned in the first area in order to obtain evidence in relation to it,

the relevant time shall be—

      (i) the time 24 hours after he leaves the place where he is detained in the first area ; or

      (ii) the time at which he arrives at the first police station to which he is taken in the second area,

whichever is the earlier.

(6) When a person who is in police detention is removed to hospital because he is in need of medical treatment, any time during which he is being questioned in hospital or on the way there or back by a police officer for the purpose of obtaining evidence relating to an offence shall be included in any period which falls to be calculated for the purposes of this Part of this Act, but any other time while he is in hospital or on his way there or back shall not be so included.

(7) Subject to subsection (8) below, a person who at the expiry of 24 hours after the relevant time is in police detention and has not been charged shall be released at that time either on bail or without bail.

(8) Subsection (7) above does not apply to a person whose detention for more than 24 hours after the relevant time has been authorised or is otherwise permitted in accordance with section 42 or 43 below.

(9) A person released under subsection (7) above shall not be re-arrested without a warrant for the offence for which he was previously arrested unless new evidence justifying a further arrest has come to light since his release.

Authorisation of continued detention.

42.—(1) Where a police officer of the rank of superintendent or above who is responsible for the police station at which a person is detained has reasonable grounds for believing that—

      (a) the detention of that person without charge is necessary to secure or preserve evidence relating to an offence for which he is under arrest or to obtain such evidence by questioning him ;

      (b) an offence for which he is under arrest is a serious arrestable offence ; and

      (c) the investigation is being conducted diligently and expeditiously,

he may authorise the keeping of that person in police detention for a period expiring at or before 36 hours after the relevant time.

(2) Where an officer such as is mentioned in subsection (1) above has authorised the keeping of a person in police detention for a period expiring less than 36 hours after the relevant time, such an officer may authorise the keeping of that person in police detention for a further period expiring not more than 36 hours after that time if the conditions specified in subsection (1) above are still satisfied when he gives the authorisation.

(3) If it is proposed to transfer a person in police detention to another police area, the officer determining whether or not to authorise keeping him in detention under subsection (1) above shall have regard to the distance and the time the journey would take.

(4) No authorisation under subsection (1) above shall be given in respect of any person—

   (a) more than 24 hours after the relevant time; or
   (b) before the second review of his detention under section 40 above has been carried out.

(5) Where an officer authorises the keeping of a person in police detention under subsection (1) above, it shall be his duty—

   (a) to inform that person of the grounds for his continued detention; and
   (b) to record the grounds in that person's custody record.

(6) Before determining whether to authorise the keeping of a person in detention under subsection (1) or (2) above, an officer shall give—

   (a) that person; or
   (b) any solicitor representing him who is available at the time when it falls to the officer to determine whether to give the authorisation,

an opportunity to make representations to him about the detention.

(7) Subject to subsection (8) below, the person in detention or his solicitor may make representations under subsection (6) above either orally or in writing.

(8) The officer to whom it falls to determine whether to give the authorisation may refuse to hear oral representations from the person in detention if he considers that he is unfit to make such representations by reason of his condition or behaviour.

(9) Where—

   (a) an officer authorises the keeping of a person in detention under subsection (1) above; and

PART IV

(b) at the time of the authorisation he has not yet exercised a right conferred on him by section 56 or 58 below,

the officer—
(i) shall inform him of that right;
(ii) shall decide whether he should be permitted to exercise it;
(iii) shall record the decision in his custody record; and
(iv) if the decision is to refuse to permit the exercise of the right, shall also record the grounds for the decision in that record.

(10) Where an officer has authorised the keeping of a person who has not been charged in detention under subsection (1) or (2) above, he shall be released from detention, either on bail or without bail, not later than 36 hours after the relevant time, unless—

(a) he has been charged with an offence; or
(b) his continued detention is authorised or otherwise permitted in accordance with section 43 below.

(11) A person released under subsection (10) above shall not be re-arrested without a warrant for the offence for which he was previously arrested unless new evidence justifying a further arrest has come to light since his release.

Warrants of further detention.

43.—(1) Where, on an application on oath made by a constable and supported by an information, a magistrates' court is satisfied that there are reasonable grounds for believing that the further detention of the person to whom the application relates is justified, it may issue a warrant of further detention authorising the keeping of that person in police detention.

(2) A court may not hear an application for a warrant of further detention unless the person to whom the application relates—

(a) has been furnished with a copy of the information; and
(b) has been brought before the court for the hearing.

(3) The person to whom the application relates shall be entitled to be legally represented at the hearing and, if he is not so represented but wishes to be so represented—

(a) the court shall adjourn the hearing to enable him to obtain representation; and
(b) he may be kept in police detention during the adjournment.

(4) A person's further detention is only justified for the purposes of this section or section 44 below if—

(a) his detention without charge is necessary to secure or preserve evidence relating to an offence for which he is under arrest or to obtain such evidence by questioning him;

(b) an offence for which he is under arrest is a serious arrestable offence; and

(c) the investigation is being conducted diligently and expeditiously.

(5) Subject to subsection (7) below, an application for a warrant of further detention may be made—

(a) at any time before the expiry of 36 hours after the relevant time; or

(b) in a case where—

(i) it is not practicable for the magistrates' court to which the application will be made to sit at the expiry of 36 hours after the relevant time; but

(ii) the court will sit during the 6 hours following the end of that period,

at any time before the expiry of the said 6 hours.

(6) In a case to which subsection (5)(b) above applies—

(a) the person to whom the application relates may be kept in police detention until the application is heard; and

(b) the custody officer shall make a note in that person's custody record—

(i) of the fact that he was kept in police detention for more than 36 hours after the relevant time; and

(ii) of the reason why he was so kept.

(7) If—

(a) an application for a warrant of further detention is made after the expiry of 36 hours after the relevant time; and

(b) it appears to the magistrates' court that it would have been reasonable for the police to make it before the expiry of that period,

the court shall dismiss the application.

(8) Where on an application such as is mentioned in subsection (1) above a magistrates' court is not satisfied that there are reasonable grounds for believing that the further detention of the person to whom the application relates is justified, it shall be its duty—

(a) to refuse the application; or

(b) to adjourn the hearing of it until a time not later than 36 hours after the relevant time.

(9) The person to whom the application relates may be kept in police detention during the adjournment.

(10) A warrant of further detention shall—
  (a) state the time at which it is issued;
  (b) authorise the keeping in police detention of the person to whom it relates for the period stated in it.

(11) Subject to subsection (12) below, the period stated in a warrant of further detention shall be such period as the magistrates' court thinks fit, having regard to the evidence before it.

(12) The period shall not be longer than 36 hours.

(13) If it is proposed to transfer a person in police detention to a police area other than that in which he is detained when the application for a warrant of further detention is made, the court hearing the application shall have regard to the distance and the time the journey would take.

(14) Any information submitted in support of an application under this section shall state—
  (a) the nature of the offence for which the person to whom the application relates has been arrested;
  (b) the general nature of the evidence on which that person was arrested;
  (c) what inquiries relating to the offence have been made by the police and what further inquiries are proposed by them;
  (d) the reasons for believing the continued detention of that person to be necessary for the purposes of such further inquiries.

(15) Where an application under this section is refused, the person to whom the application relates shall forthwith be charged or, subject to subsection (16) below, released, either on bail or without bail.

(16) A person need not be released under subsection (15) above—
  (a) before the expiry of 24 hours after the relevant time; or
  (b) before the expiry of any longer period for which his continued detention is or has been authorised under section 42 above.

(17) Where an application under this section is refused, no further application shall be made under this section in respect of the person to whom the refusal relates, unless supported by evidence which has come to light since the refusal.

(18) Where a warrant of further detention is issued, the person to whom it relates shall be released from police detention, either on bail or without bail, upon or before the expiry of the warrant unless he is charged.

(19) A person released under subsection (18) above shall not be re-arrested without a warrant for the offence for which he was previously arrested unless new evidence justifying a further arrest has come to light since his release.

44.—(1) On an application on oath made by a constable and supported by an information a magistrates' court may extend a warrant of further detention issued under section 43 above if it is satisfied that there are reasonable grounds for believing that the further detention of the person to whom the application relates is justified.

Extension of warrants of further detention.

(2) Subject to subsection (3) below, the period for which a warrant of further detention may be extended shall be such period as the court thinks fit, having regard to the evidence before it.

(3) The period shall not—
   (a) be longer than 36 hours; or
   (b) end later than 96 hours after the relevant time.

(4) Where a warrant of further detention has been extended under subsection (1) above, or further extended under this subsection, for a period ending before 96 hours after the relevant time, on an application such as is mentioned in that subsection a magistrates' court may further extend the warrant if it is satisfied as there mentioned; and subsections (2) and (3) above apply to such further extensions as they apply to extensions under subsection (1) above.

(5) A warrant of further detention shall, if extended or further extended under this section, be endorsed with a note of the period of the extension.

(6) Subsections (2), (3) and (14) of section 43 above shall apply to an application made under this section as they apply to an application made under that section.

(7) Where an application under this section is refused, the person to whom the application relates shall forthwith be charged or, subject to subsection (8) below, released, either on bail or without bail.

(8) A person need not be released under subsection (7) above before the expiry of any period for which a warrant of further detention issued in relation to him has been extended or further extended on an earlier application made under this section.

45.—(1) In sections 43 and 44 of this Act " magistrates' court " means a court consisting of two or more justices of the peace sitting otherwise than in open court.

Detention before charge— supplementary.

(2) Any reference in this Part of this Act to a period of time or a time of day is to be treated as approximate only.

Detention—miscellaneous

46.—(1) Where a person—
  (a) is charged with an offence; and
  (b) after being charged—
    (i) is kept in police detention; or
    (ii) is detained by a local authority in pursuance of arrangements made under section 38(6) above,

he shall be brought before a magistrates' court in accordance with the provisions of this section.

(2) If he is to be brought before a magistrates' court for the petty sessions area in which the police station at which he was charged is situated, he shall be brought before such a court as soon as is practicable and in any event not later than the first sitting after he is charged with the offence.

(3) If no magistrates' court for that area is due to sit either on the day on which he is charged or on the next day, the custody officer for the police station at which he was charged shall inform the clerk to the justices for the area that there is a person in the area to whom subsection (2) above applies.

(4) If the person charged is to be brought before a magistrates' court for a petty sessions area other than that in which the police station at which he was charged is situated, he shall be removed to that area as soon as is practicable and brought before such a court as soon as is practicable after his arrival in the area and in any event not later than the first sitting of a magistrates' court for that area after his arrival in the area.

(5) If no magistrates' court for that area is due to sit either on the day on which he arrives in the area or on the next day—
  (a) he shall be taken to a police station in the area; and
  (b) the custody officer at that station shall inform the clerk to the justices for the area that there is a person in the area to whom subsection (4) applies.

(6) Subject to subsection (8) below, where a clerk to the justices for a petty sessions area has been informed—
  (a) under subsection (3) above that there is a person in the area to whom subsection (2) above applies; or
  (b) under subsection (5) above that there is a person in the area to whom subsection (4) above applies,

the clerk shall arrange for a magistrates' court to sit not later than the day next following the relevant day.

(7) In this section " the relevant day "—
- (a) in relation to a person who is to be brought before a magistrates' court for the petty sessions area in which the police station at which he was charged is situated, means the day on which he was charged ; and
- (b) in relation to a person who is to be brought before a magistrates' court for any other petty sessions area, means the day on which he arrives in the area.

(8) Where the day next following the relevant day is Christmas Day, Good Friday or a Sunday, the duty of the clerk under subsection (6) above is a duty to arrange for a magistrates' court to sit not later than the first day after the relevant day which is not one of those days.

(9) Nothing in this section requires a person who is in hospital to be brought before a court if he is not well enough.

47.—(1) Subject to subsection (2) below, a release on bail of a person under this Part of this Act shall be a release on bail granted in accordance with the Bail Act 1976.

(2) Nothing in the Bail Act 1976 shall prevent the re-arrest without warrant of a person released on bail subject to a duty to attend at a police station if new evidence justifying a further arrest has come to light since his release.

(3) Subject to subsection (4) below, in this Part of this Act references to " bail " are references to bail subject to a duty—
- (a) to appear before a magistrates' court at such time and such place ; or
- (b) to attend at such police station at such time,

as the custody officer may appoint.

(4) Where a custody officer has granted bail to a person subject to a duty to appear at a police station, the custody officer may give notice in writing to that person that his attendance at the police station is not required.

(5) Where a person arrested for an offence who was released on bail subject to a duty to attend at a police station so attends, he may be detained without charge in connection with that offence only if the custody officer at the police station has reasonable grounds for believing that his detention is necessary—
- (a) to secure or preserve evidence relating to the offence ; or
- (b) to obtain such evidence by questioning him.

(6) Where a person is detained under subsection (5) above, any time during which he was in police detention prior to being

PART IV granted bail shall be included as part of any period which falls to be calculated under this Part of this Act.

(7) Where a person who was released on bail subject to a duty to attend at a police station is re-arrested, the provisions of this Part of this Act shall apply to him as they apply to a person arrested for the first time.

1980 c. 43.
(8) In the Magistrates' Courts Act 1980—
   (a) the following section shall be substituted for section 43—

"Bail on arrest
43.—(1) Where a person has been granted bail under the Police and Criminal Evidence Act 1984 subject to a duty to appear before a magistrates' court, the court before which he is to appear may appoint a later time as the time at which he is to appear and may enlarge the recognizances of any sureties for him at that time.

(2) The recognizance of any surety for any person granted bail subject to a duty to attend at a police station may be enforced as if it were conditioned for his appearance before a magistrates' court for the petty sessions area in which the police station named in the recognizance is situated." ; and

   (b) the following subsection shall be substituted for section 117(3)—

"(3) Where a warrant has been endorsed for bail under subsection (1) above—
   (a) where the person arrested is to be released on bail on his entering into a recognizance without sureties, it shall not be necessary to take him to a police station, but if he is so taken, he shall be released from custody on his entering into the recognizance ; and
   (b) where he is to be released on his entering into a recognizance with sureties, he shall be taken to a police station on his arrest, and the custody officer there shall (subject to his approving any surety tendered in compliance with the endorsement) release him from custody as directed in the endorsement.".

Remands to police detention.
48. In section 128 of the Magistrates' Courts Act 1980—
   (a) in subsection (7) for the words " the custody of a constable " there shall be substituted the words " detention at a police station " ;

(b) after subsection (7) there shall be inserted the following subsection—

"(8) Where a person is committed to detention at a police station under subsection (7) above—

(a) he shall not be kept in such detention unless there is a need for him to be so detained for the purposes of inquiries into other offences;

(b) if kept in such detention, he shall be brought back before the magistrates' court which committed him as soon as that need ceases;

(c) he shall be treated as a person in police detention to whom the duties under section 39 of the Police and Criminal Evidence Act 1984 (responsibilities in relation to persons detained) relate;

(d) his detention shall be subject to periodic review at the times set out in section 40 of that Act (review of police detention).".

49.—(1) In subsection (1) of section 67 of the Criminal Justice Act 1967 (computation of custodial sentences) for the words from "period", in the first place where it occurs, to "the offender" there shall be substituted the words "relevant period, but where he".

Police detention to count towards custodial sentence.
1967 c. 80.

(2) The following subsection shall be inserted after that subsection—

"(1A) In subsection (1) above "relevant period" means—

(a) any period during which the offender was in police detention in connection with the offence for which the sentence was passed; or

(b) any period during which he was in custody—

(i) by reason only of having been committed to custody by an order of a court made in connection with any proceedings relating to that sentence or the offence for which it was passed or any proceedings from which those proceedings arose; or

(ii) by reason of his having been so committed and having been concurrently detained otherwise than by order of a court.".

(3) The following subsections shall be added after subsection (6) of that section—

"(7) A person is in police detention for the purposes of this section—

(a) at any time when he is in police detention for the

PART IV

1984 c. 8.

purposes of the Police and Criminal Evidence Act 1984; and

(b) at any time when he is detained under section 12 of the Prevention of Terrorism (Temporary Provisions) Act 1984.

(8) No period of police detention shall be taken into account under this section unless it falls after the coming into force of section 49 of the Police and Criminal Evidence Act 1984.".

Records of detention.

50.—(1) Each police force shall keep written records showing on an annual basis—

(a) the number of persons kept in police detention for more than 24 hours and subsequently released without charge;

(b) the number of applications for warrants of further detention and the results of the applications; and

(c) in relation to each warrant of further detention—

(i) the period of further detention authorised by it;

(ii) the period which the person named in it spent in police detention on its authority; and

(iii) whether he was charged or released without charge.

(2) Every annual report—

1964 c. 48.

(a) under section 12 of the Police Act 1964; or

(b) made by the Commissioner of Police of the Metropolis,

shall contain information about the matters mentioned in subsection (1) above in respect of the period to which the report relates.

Savings.

51. Nothing in this Part of this Act shall affect—

1971 c. 77.

(a) the powers conferred on immigration officers by section 4 of and Schedule 2 to the Immigration Act 1971 (administrative provisions as to control on entry etc.);

(b) the powers conferred by or by virtue of section 12 or 13 of the Prevention of Terrorism (Temporary Provisions) Act 1984 (powers of arrest and detention and control of entry and procedure for removal);

(c) any duty of a police officer under—

1955 c. 18.

(i) section 129, 190 or 202 of the Army Act 1955 (duties of governors of prisons and others to receive prisoners, deserters, absentees and persons under escort);

(ii) section 129, 190 or 202 of the Air Force Act 1955 (duties of governors of prisons and others to receive prisoners, deserters, absentees and persons under escort);

PART IV
1955 c. 19.

(iii) section 107 of the Naval Discipline Act 1957 (duties of governors of civil prisons etc.); or

1957 c. 53.

(iv) paragraph 5 of Schedule 5 to the Reserve Forces Act 1980 (duties of governors of civil prisons); or

1980 c. 9.

(d) any right of a person in police detention to apply for a writ of habeas corpus or other prerogative remedy.

52. This Part of this Act does not apply to a child (as for the time being defined for the purposes of the Children and Young Persons Act 1969) who is arrested without a warrant otherwise than for homicide and to whom section 28(4) and (5) of that Act accordingly apply.

Children.
1969 c. 54.

PART V

QUESTIONING AND TREATMENT OF PERSONS BY POLICE

53.—(1) Subject to subsection (2) below, there shall cease to have effect any Act (including a local Act) passed before this Act in so far as it authorises—

Abolition of certain powers of constables to search persons.

(a) any search by a constable of a person in police detention at a police station; or

(b) an intimate search of a person by a constable;

and any rule of common law which authorises a search such as is mentioned in paragraph (a) or (b) above is abolished.

(2) Nothing in subsection (1)(a) above shall affect paragraph 6(2) of Schedule 3 to the Prevention of Terrorism (Temporary Provisions) Act 1984.

1984 c. 8.

54.—(1) The custody officer at a police station shall ascertain and record or cause to be recorded everything which a person has with him when he is—

Searches of detained persons.

(a) brought to the station after being arrested elsewhere or after being committed to custody by an order or sentence of a court; or

(b) arrested at the station after—

(i) having attended voluntarily there; or

(ii) having accompanied a constable there without having been arrested.

PART V

(2) In the case of an arrested person the record shall be made as part of his custody record.

(3) Subject to subsection (4) below, a custody officer may seize and retain any such thing or cause any such thing to be seized and retained.

(4) Clothes and personal effects may only be seized if the custody officer—
- (a) believes that the person from whom they are seized may use them—
  - (i) to cause physical injury to himself or any other person;
  - (ii) to damage property;
  - (iii) to interfere with evidence; or
  - (iv) to assist him to escape; or
- (b) has reasonable grounds for believing that they may be evidence relating to an offence.

(5) Where anything is seized, the person from whom it is seized shall be told the reason for the seizure unless he is—
- (a) violent or likely to become violent; or
- (b) incapable of understanding what is said to him.

(6) Subject to subsection (7) below, a person may be searched if the custody officer considers it necessary to enable him to carry out his duty under subsection (1) above and to the extent that the custody officer considers necessary for that purpose.

(7) An intimate search may not be conducted under this section.

(8) A search under this section shall be carried out by a constable.

(9) The constable carrying out a search shall be of the same sex as the person searched.

Intimate searches.

55.—(1) Subject to the following provisions of this section, if an officer of at least the rank of superintendent has reasonable grounds for believing—
- (a) that a person who has been arrested and is in police detention may have concealed on him anything which—
  - (i) he could use to cause physical injury to himself or others; and
  - (ii) he might so use while he is in police detention or in the custody of a court; or
- (b) that such a person—
  - (i) may have a Class A drug concealed on him; and

(ii) was in possession of it with the appropriate criminal intent before his arrest,

he may authorise such a search of that person.

(2) An officer may not authorise an intimate search of a person for anything unless he has reasonable grounds for believing that it cannot be found without his being intimately searched.

(3) An officer may give an authorisation under subsection (1) above orally or in writing but, if he gives it orally, he shall confirm it in writing as soon as is practicable.

(4) An intimate search which is only a drug offence search shall be by way of examination by a suitably qualified person.

(5) Except as provided by subsection (4) above, an intimate search shall be by way of examination by a suitably qualified person unless an officer of at least the rank of superintendent considers that this is not practicable.

(6) An intimate search which is not carried out as mentioned in subsection (5) above shall be carried out by a constable.

(7) A constable may not carry out an intimate search of a person of the opposite sex.

(8) No intimate search may be carried out except—
 (a) at a police station;
 (b) at a hospital;
 (c) at a registered medical practitioner's surgery; or
 (d) at some other place used for medical purposes.

(9) An intimate search which is only a drug offence search may not be carried out at a police station.

(10) If an intimate search of a person is carried out, the custody record relating to him shall state—
 (a) which parts of his body were searched; and
 (b) why they were searched.

(11) The information required to be recorded by subsection (10) above shall be recorded as soon as practicable after the completion of the search.

(12) The custody officer at a police station may seize and retain anything which is found on an intimate search of a person, or cause any such thing to be seized and retained—
 (a) if he believes that the person from whom it is seized may use it—
  (i) to cause physical injury to himself or any other person;
  (ii) to damage property;

(iii) to interfere with evidence ; or

(iv) to assist him to escape ; or

(b) if he has reasonable grounds for believing that it may be evidence relating to an offence.

(13) Where anything is seized under this section, the person from whom it is seized shall be told the reason for the seizure unless he is—

(a) violent or likely to become violent ; or

(b) incapable of understanding what is said to him.

(14) Every annual report—

(a) under section 12 of the Police Act 1964 ; or

(b) made by the Commissioner of Police of the Metropolis,

shall contain information about searches under this section which have been carried out in the area to which the report relates during the period to which it relates.

(15) The information about such searches shall include—

(a) the total number of searches ;

(b) the number of searches conducted by way of examination by a suitably qualified person ;

(c) the number of searches not so conducted but conducted in the presence of such a person ; and

(d) the result of the searches carried out.

(16) The information shall also include, as separate items—

(a) the total number of drug offence searches ; and

(b) the result of those searches.

(17) In this section—

"the appropriate criminal intent" means an intent to commit an offence under—

(a) section 5(3) of the Misuse of Drugs Act 1971 (possession of controlled drug with intent to supply to another) ; or

(b) section 68(2) of the Customs and Excise Management Act 1979 (exportation etc. with intent to evade a prohibition or restriction) ;

"Class A drug" has the meaning assigned to it by section 2(1)(b) of the Misuse of Drugs Act 1971 ;

"drug offence search" means an intimate search for a Class A drug which an officer has authorised by virtue of subsection (1)(b) above ; and

"suitably qualified person" means—

(a) a registered medical practitioner ; or

(b) a registered nurse.

56.—(1) Where a person has been arrested and is being held in custody in a police station or other premises, he shall be entitled, if he so requests, to have one friend or relative or other person who is known to him or who is likely to take an interest in his welfare told, as soon as is practicable except to the extent that delay is permitted by this section, that he has been arrested and is being detained there.

PART V
Right to have someone informed when arrested.

(2) Delay is only permitted—
  (a) in the case of a person who is in police detention for a serious arrestable offence; and
  (b) if an officer of at least the rank of superintendent authorises it.

(3) In any case the person in custody must be permitted to exercise the right conferred by subsection (1) above within 36 hours from the relevant time, as defined in section 41(2) above.

(4) An officer may give an authorisation under subsection (2) above orally or in writing but, if he gives it orally, he shall confirm it in writing as soon as is practicable.

(5) An officer may only authorise delay where he has reasonable grounds for believing that telling the named person of the arrest—
  (a) will lead to interference with or harm to evidence connected with a serious arrestable offence or interference with or physical injury to other persons; or
  (b) will lead to the alerting of other persons suspected of having committed such an offence but not yet arrested for it; or
  (c) will hinder the recovery of any property obtained as a result of such an offence.

(6) If a delay is authorised—
  (a) the detained person shall be told the reason for it; and
  (b) the reason shall be noted on his custody record.

(7) The duties imposed by subsection (6) above shall be performed as soon as is practicable.

(8) The rights conferred by this section on a person detained at a police station or other premises are exercisable whenever he is transferred from one place to another; and this section applies to each subsequent occasion on which they are exercisable as it applies to the first such occasion.

(9) There may be no further delay in permitting the exercise of the right conferred by subsection (1) above once the reason for authorising delay ceases to subsist.

PART V

(10) In the foregoing provisions of this section references to a person who has been arrested include references to a person who has been detained under the terrorism provisions and "arrest" includes detention under those provisions.

(11) In its application to a person who has been arrested or detained under the terrorism provisions—

(a) subsection (2)(a) above shall have effect as if for the words "for a serious arrestable offence" there were substituted the words "under the terrorism provisions";

(b) subsection (3) above shall have effect as if for the words from "within" onwards there were substituted the words "before the end of the period beyond which he may no longer be detained without the authority of the Secretary of State"; and

(c) subsection (5) above shall have effect as if at the end there were added "or

(d) will lead to interference with the gathering of information about the commission, preparation or instigation of acts of terrorism; or

(e) by alerting any person, will make it more difficult—

(i) to prevent an act of terrorism; or

(ii) to secure the apprehension, prosecution or conviction of any person in connection with the commission, preparation or instigation of an act of terrorism.".

Additional rights of children and young persons.
1933 c. 12.

57. The following subsections shall be substituted for section 34(2) of the Children and Young Persons Act 1933—

" (2) Where a child or young person is in police detention, such steps as are practicable shall be taken to ascertain the identity of a person responsible for his welfare.

(3) If it is practicable to ascertain the identity of a person responsible for the welfare of the child or young person, that person shall be informed, unless it is not practicable to do so—

(a) that the child or young person has been arrested;

(b) why he has been arrested; and

(c) where he is being detained.

(4) Where information falls to be given under subsection (3) above, it shall be given as soon as it is practicable to do so.

(5) For the purposes of this section the persons who may be responsible for the welfare of a child or young person are—

(a) his parent or guardian; or

(b) any other person who has for the time being assumed responsibility for his welfare.

(6) If it is practicable to give a person responsible for the welfare of the child or young person the information required by subsection (3) above, that person shall be given it as soon as it is practicable to do so.

(7) If it appears that at the time of his arrest a supervision order, as defined in section 11 of the Children and Young Persons Act 1969, is in force in respect of him, the person responsible for his supervision shall also be informed as described in subsection (3) above as soon as it is reasonably practicable to do so.

1969 c. 54.

(8) The reference to a parent or guardian in subsection (5) above is—

(a) in the case of a child or young person in the care of a local authority, a reference to that authority; and

(b) in the case of a child or young person in the care of a voluntary organisation in which parental rights and duties with respect to him are vested by virtue of a resolution under section 64(1) of the Child Care Act 1980, a reference to that organisation.

1980 c. 5.

(9) The rights conferred on a child or young person by subsections (2) to (8) above are in addition to his rights under section 56 of the Police and Criminal Evidence Act 1984.

(10) The reference in subsection (2) above to a child or young person who is in police detention includes a reference to a child or young person who has been detained under the terrorism provisions; and in subsection (3) above " arrest " includes such detention.

(11) In subsection (10) above " the terrorism provisions " has the meaning assigned to it by section 65 of the Police and Criminal Evidence Act 1984 ".

58.—(1) A person arrested and held in custody in a police station or other premises shall be entitled, if he so requests, to consult a solicitor privately at any time.

Access to legal advice.

(2) Subject to subsection (3) below, a request under subsection (1) above and the time at which it was made shall be recorded in the custody record.

(3) Such a request need not be recorded in the custody record of a person who makes it at a time while he is at a court after being charged with an offence.

(4) If a person makes such a request, he must be permitted to consult a solicitor as soon as is practicable except to the extent that delay is permitted by this section.

(5) In any case he must be permitted to consult a solicitor within 36 hours from the relevant time, as defined in section 41(2) above.

(6) Delay in compliance with a request is only permitted—
  (a) in the case of a person who is in police detention for a serious arrestable offence ; and
  (b) if an officer of at least the rank of superintendent authorises it.

(7) An officer may give an authorisation under subsection (6) above orally or in writing but, if he gives it orally, he shall confirm it in writing as soon as is practicable.

(8) An officer may only authorise delay where he has reasonable grounds for believing that the exercise of the right conferred by subsection (1) above at the time when the person detained desires to exercise it—
  (a) will lead to interference with or harm to evidence connected with a serious arrestable offence or interference with or physical injury to other persons ; or
  (b) will lead to the alerting of other persons suspected of having committed such an offence but not yet arrested for it ; or
  (c) will hinder the recovery of any property obtained as a result of such an offence.

(9) If delay is authorised—
  (a) the detained person shall be told the reason for it; and
  (b) the reason shall be noted on his custody record.

(10) The duties imposed by subsection (9) above shall be performed as soon as is practicable.

(11) There may be no further delay in permitting the exercise of the right conferred by subsection (1) above once the reason for authorising delay ceases to subsist.

(12) The reference in subsection (1) above to a person arrested includes a reference to a person who has been detained under the terrorism provisions.

(13) In the application of this section to a person who has been arrested or detained under the terrorism provisions—
  (a) subsection (5) above shall have effect as if for the words from " within " onwards there were substituted the

words " before the end of the period beyond which he may no longer be detained without the authority of the Secretary of State ";

(b) subsection (6)(a) above shall have effect as if for the words " for a serious arrestable offence " there were substituted the words " under the terrorism provisions "; and

(c) subsection (8) above shall have effect as if at the end there were added " or

(d) will lead to interference with the gathering of information about the commission, preparation or instigation of acts of terrorism; or

(e) by alerting any person, will make it more difficult—

(i) to prevent an act of terrorism; or

(ii) to secure the apprehension, prosecution or conviction of any person in connection with the commission, preparation or instigation of an act of terrorism.".

(14) If an officer of appropriate rank has reasonable grounds for believing that, unless he gives a direction under subsection (15) below, the exercise by a person arrested or detained under the terrorism provisions of the right conferred by subsection (1) above will have any of the consequences specified in subsection (8) above (as it has effect by virtue of subsection (13) above), he may give a direction under that subsection.

(15) A direction under this subsection is a direction that a person desiring to exercise the right conferred by subsection (1) above may only consult a solicitor in the sight and hearing of a qualified officer of the uniformed branch of the force of which the officer giving the direction is a member.

(16) An officer is qualified for the purpose of subsection (15) above if—

(a) he is of at least the rank of inspector; and

(b) in the opinion of the officer giving the direction he has no connection with the case.

(17) An officer is of appropriate rank to give a direction under subsection (15) above if he is of at least the rank of Commander or Assistant Chief Constable.

(18) A direction under subsection (15) above shall cease to have effect once the reason for giving it ceases to subsist.

PART V
Legal aid for persons at police stations.
1982 c. 44.

59. In section 1 of the Legal Aid Act 1982 (duty solicitors)—

(a) in subsection (1) the following paragraph shall be inserted after paragraph (a)—

"(aa) for the making, by such committees, of arrangements whereby advice and assistance under section 1 of the principal Act is provided for persons—

(i) such as are mentioned in section 29 of the Police and Criminal Evidence Act 1984; or

(ii) arrested and held in custody who—

(i) exercise the right to consult a solicitor conferred on them by section 58(1) of that Act; or

(ii) are permitted to consult a representative of a solicitor; and ";

(b) in paragraph (b) after the word " representation " there shall be inserted the words " or advice and assistance ";

(c) the following subsection shall be inserted after that subsection—

" (1A) A scheme under section 15 of the principal Act which relates to advice and representation at magistrates' courts may provide that arrangements made under it may be so framed as to preclude solicitors from providing such advice and representation if they do not also provide advice and assistance in pursuance of arrangements made by virtue of a scheme under that section which relates to the provision of advice and assistance for persons such as are mentioned in section 29 of the Police and Criminal Evidence Act 1984 and for persons arrested and held in custody."; and

(d) in subsection (5) for the words " such arrangements as are mentioned in subsection (1) above " there shall be substituted the words " arrangements made under subsection (1) above for the provision of advice and representation at the court ".

Tape-recording of interviews.

60.—(1) It shall be the duty of the Secretary of State—

(a) to issue a code of practice in connection with the tape-recording of interviews of persons suspected of the commission of criminal offences which are held by police officers at police stations; and

(b) to make an order requiring the tape-recording of interviews of persons suspected of the commission of criminal offences, or of such descriptions of criminal offences as may be specified in the order, which are so held, in accordance with the code as it has effect for the time being.

PART V

(2) An order under subsection (1) above shall be made by statutory instrument and shall be subject to annulment in pursuance of a resolution of either House of Parliament.

61.—(1) Except as provided by this section no person's fingerprints may be taken without the appropriate consent.

Fingerprinting.

(2) Consent to the taking of a person's fingerprints must be in writing if it is given at a time when he is at a police station.

(3) The fingerprints of a person detained at a police station may be taken without the appropriate consent—

(a) if an officer of at least the rank of superintendent authorises them to be taken; or

(b) if—

(i) he has been charged with a recordable offence or informed that he will be reported for such an offence; and

(ii) he has not had his fingerprints taken in the course of the investigation of the offence by the police.

(4) An officer may only give an authorisation under subsection (3)(a) above if he has reasonable grounds—

(a) for suspecting the involvement of the person whose fingerprints are to be taken in a criminal offence; and

(b) for believing that his fingerprints will tend to confirm or disprove his involvement.

(5) An officer may give an authorisation under subsection (3)(a) above orally or in writing but, if he gives it orally, he shall confirm it in writing as soon as is practicable.

(6) Any person's fingerprints may be taken without the appropriate consent if he has been convicted of a recordable offence.

(7) In a case where by virtue of subsection (3) or (6) above a person's fingerprints are taken without the appropriate consent—

(a) he shall be told the reason before his fingerprints are taken; and

(b) the reason shall be recorded as soon as is practicable after the fingerprints are taken.

(8) If he is detained at a police station when the fingerprints are taken, the reason for taking them shall be recorded on his custody record.

PART V

1971 c. 77.

(9) Nothing in this section—

(a) affects any power conferred by paragraph 18(2) of Schedule 2 to the Immigration Act 1971; or

(b) applies to a person arrested or detained under the terrorism provisions.

Intimate samples

62.—(1) An intimate sample may be taken from a person in police detention only—

(a) if a police officer of at least the rank of superintendent authorises it to be taken; and

(b) if the appropriate consent is given.

(2) An officer may only give an authorisation if he has reasonable grounds—

(a) for suspecting the involvement of the person from whom the sample is to be taken in a serious arrestable offence; and

(b) for believing that the sample will tend to confirm or disprove his involvement.

(3) An officer may give an authorisation under subsection (1) above orally or in writing but, if he gives it orally, he shall confirm it in writing as soon as is practicable.

(4) The appropriate consent must be given in writing.

(5) Where—

(a) an authorisation has been given; and

(b) it is proposed that an intimate sample shall be taken in pursuance of the authorisation,

an officer shall inform the person from whom the sample is to be taken—

(i) of the giving of the authorisation; and

(ii) of the grounds for giving it.

(6) The duty imposed by subsection (5)(ii) above includes a duty to state the nature of the offence in which it is suspected that the person from whom the sample is to be taken has been involved.

(7) If an intimate sample is taken from a person—

(a) the authorisation by virtue of which it was taken;

(b) the grounds for giving the authorisation; and

(c) the fact that the appropriate consent was given,

shall be recorded as soon as is practicable after the sample is taken.

(8) If an intimate sample is taken from a person detained at a police station, the matters required to be recorded by subsection (7) above shall be recorded in his custody record.

(9) An intimate sample, other than a sample of urine or saliva, may only be taken from a person by a registered medical practitioner.

(10) Where the appropriate consent to the taking of an intimate sample from a person was refused without good cause, in any proceedings against that person for an offence—

(a) the court, in determining—

(i) whether to commit that person for trial; or

(ii) whether there is a case to answer; and

(b) the court or jury, in determining whether that person is guilty of the offence charged,

may draw such inferences from the refusal as appear proper; and the refusal may, on the basis of such inferences, be treated as, or as capable of amounting to, corroboration of any evidence against the person in relation to which the refusal is material.

(11) Nothing in this section affects sections 5 to 12 of the Road Traffic Act 1972.

1972 c. 20.

63.—(1) Except as provided by this section, a non-intimate sample may not be taken from a person without the appropriate consent.

Other samples.

(2) Consent to the taking of a non-intimate sample must be given in writing.

(3) A non-intimate sample may be taken from a person without the appropriate consent if—

(a) he is in police detention or is being held in custody by the police on the authority of a court; and

(b) an officer of at least the rank of superintendent authorises it to be taken without the appropriate consent.

(4) An officer may only give an authorisation under subsection (3) above if he has reasonable grounds—

(a) for suspecting the involvement of the person from whom the sample is to be taken in a serious arrestable offence; and

(b) for believing that the sample will tend to confirm or disprove his involvement.

(5) An officer may give an authorisation under subsection (3) above orally or in writing but, if he gives it orally, he shall confirm it in writing as soon as is practicable.

(6) Where—

(a) an authorisation has been given; and

PART V   (*b*) it is proposed that a non-intimate sample shall be taken in pursuance of the authorisation,

an officer shall inform the person from whom the sample is to be taken—

    (i) of the giving of the authorisation; and

    (ii) of the grounds for giving it.

(7) The duty imposed by subsection (6)(ii) above includes a duty to state the nature of the offence in which it is suspected that the person from whom the sample is to be taken has been involved.

(8) If a non-intimate sample is taken from a person by virtue of subsection (3) above—

    (*a*) the authorisation by virtue of which it was taken; and

    (*b*) the grounds for giving the authorisation,

shall be recorded as soon as is practicable after the sample is taken.

(9) If a non-intimate sample is taken from a person detained at a police station, the matters required to be recorded by subsection (8) above shall be recorded in his custody record.

Destruction of fingerprints and samples.

64.—(1) If—

    (*a*) fingerprints or samples are taken from a person in connection with the investigation of an offence; and

    (*b*) he is cleared of that offence,

they must be destroyed as soon as is practicable after the conclusion of the proceedings.

(2) If—

    (*a*) fingerprints or samples are taken from a person in connection with such an investigation; and

    (*b*) it is decided that he shall not be prosecuted for the offence and he has not admitted it and been dealt with by way of being cautioned by a constable,

they must be destroyed as soon as is practicable after that decision is taken.

(3) If—

    (*a*) fingerprints or samples are taken from a person in connection with the investigation of an offence; and

    (*b*) that person is not suspected of having committed the offence,

they must be destroyed as soon as they have fulfilled the purpose for which they were taken.

(4) Proceedings which are discontinued are to be treated as concluded for the purposes of this section.

(5) If fingerprints are destroyed, any copies of them shall also be destroyed.

(6) A person who asks to be allowed to witness the destruction of his fingerprints or copies of them shall have a right to witness it.

(7) Nothing in this section—
   (a) affects any power conferred by paragraph 18(2) of Schedule 2 to the Immigration Act 1971; or
   (b) applies to a person arrested or detained under the terrorism provisions.

65. In this Part of this Act—
   "appropriate consent" means—
      (a) in relation to a person who has attained the age of 17 years, the consent of that person;
      (b) in relation to a person who has not attained that age but has attained the age of 14 years, the consent of that person and his parent or guardian; and
      (c) in relation to a person who has not attained the age of 14 years, the consent of his parent or guardian;
   "fingerprints" includes palm prints;
   "intimate sample" means a sample of blood, semen or any other tissue fluid, urine, saliva or pubic hair, or a swab taken from a person's body orifice;
   "non-intimate sample" means—
      (a) a sample of hair other than pubic hair;
      (b) a sample taken from a nail or from under a nail;
      (c) a swab taken from any part of a person's body other than a body orifice;
      (d) a footprint or a similar impression of any part of a person's body other than a part of his hand;
   "the terrorism provisions" means—
      (a) section 12(1) of the Prevention of Terrorism (Temporary Provisions) Act 1984; and
      (b) any provision conferring a power of arrest or detention and contained in an order under section 13 of that Act; and
   "terrorism" has the meaning assigned to it by section 14(1) of that Act.

Part VI

Codes of Practice—General

Codes of practice.

66. The Secretary of State shall issue codes of practice in connection with—

(a) the exercise by police officers of statutory powers—

(i) to search a person without first arresting him; or

(ii) to search a vehicle without making an arrest;

(b) the detention, treatment, questioning and identification of persons by police officers;

(c) searches of premises by police officers; and

(d) the seizure of property found by police officers on persons or premises.

Codes of practice—supplementary.

67.—(1) When the Secretary of State proposes to issue a code of practice to which this section applies, he shall prepare and publish a draft of that code, shall consider any representations made to him about the draft and may modify the draft accordingly.

(2) This section applies to a code of practice under section 60 or 66 above.

(3) The Secretary of State shall lay before both Houses of Parliament a draft of any code of practice prepared by him under this section.

(4) When the Secretary of State has laid the draft of a code before Parliament, he may bring the code into operation by order made by statutory instrument.

(5) No order under subsection (4) above shall have effect until approved by a resolution of each House of Parliament.

(6) An order bringing a code of practice into operation may contain such transitional provisions or savings as appear to the Secretary of State to be necessary or expedient in connection with the code of practice thereby brought into operation.

(7) The Secretary of State may from time to time revise the whole or any part of a code of practice to which this section applies and issue that revised code; and the foregoing provisions of this section shall apply (with appropriate modifications) to such a revised code as they apply to the first issue of a code.

(8) A police officer shall be liable to disciplinary proceedings for a failure to comply with any provision of such a code, unless such proceedings are precluded by section 104 below.

(9) Persons other than police officers who are charged with the duty of investigating offences or charging offenders shall in the discharge of that duty have regard to any relevant provision of such a code.

(10) A failure on the part—
- (a) of a police officer to comply with any provision of such a code ; or
- (b) of any person other than a police officer who is charged with the duty of investigating offences or charging offenders to have regard to any relevant provision of such a code in the discharge of that duty,

shall not of itself render him liable to any criminal or civil proceedings.

(11) In all criminal and civil proceedings any such code shall be admissible in evidence ; and if any provision of such a code appears to the court or tribunal conducting the proceedings to be relevant to any question arising in the proceedings it shall be taken into account in determining that question.

(12) In this section " criminal proceedings " includes—
- (a) proceedings in the United Kingdom or elsewhere before a court-martial constituted under the Army Act 1955, the Air Force Act 1955 or the Naval Discipline Act 1957 or a disciplinary court constituted under section 50 of the said Act of 1957 ;
- (b) proceedings before the Courts-Martial Appeal Court; and
- (c) proceedings before a Standing Civilian Court.

1955 c. 18.
1955 c. 19.
1957 c. 53.

Part VII

Documentary Evidence in Criminal Proceedings

68.—(1) Subject to section 69 below, a statement in a document shall be admissible in any proceedings as evidence of any fact stated therein of which direct oral evidence would be admissible if—

Evidence from documentary records.

- (a) the document is or forms part of a record compiled by a person acting under a duty from information supplied by a person (whether acting under a duty or not) who had, or may reasonably be supposed to have had, personal knowledge of the matters dealt with in that information ; and
- (b) any condition relating to the person who supplied the information which is specified in subsection (2) below is satisfied.

PART VII

(2) The conditions mentioned in subsection (1)(*b*) above are—

(*a*) that the person who supplied the information—

(i) is dead or by reason of his bodily or mental condition unfit to attend as a witness;

(ii) is outside the United Kingdom and it is not reasonably practicable to secure his attendance; or

(iii) cannot reasonably be expected (having regard to the time which has elapsed since he supplied or acquired the information and to all the circumstances) to have any recollection of the matters dealt with in that information;

(*b*) that all reasonable steps have been taken to identify the person who supplied the information but that he cannot be identified; and

(*c*) that, the identity of the person who supplied the information being known, all reasonable steps have been taken to find him, but that he cannot be found.

(3) Nothing in this section shall prejudice the admissibility of any evidence that would be admissible apart from this section.

Evidence from computer records.

69.—(1) In any proceedings, a statement in a document produced by a computer shall not be admissible as evidence of any fact stated therein unless it is shown—

(*a*) that there are no reasonable grounds for believing that the statement is inaccurate because of improper use of the computer;

(*b*) that at all material times the computer was operating properly, or if not, that any respect in which it was not operating properly or was out of operation was not such as to affect the production of the document or the accuracy of its contents; and

(*c*) that any relevant conditions specified in rules of court under subsection (2) below are satisfied.

(2) Provision may be made by rules of court requiring that in any proceedings where it is desired to give a statement in evidence by virtue of this section such information concerning the statement as may be required by the rules shall be provided in such form and at such time as may be so required.

Provisions supplementary to sections 68 and 69.

70.—(1) Part I of Schedule 3 to this Act shall have effect for the purpose of supplementing section 68 above.

(2) Part II of that Schedule shall have effect for the purpose of supplementing section 69 above.

(3) Part III of that Schedule shall have effect for the purpose of supplementing both sections.

71. In any proceedings the contents of a document may (whether or not the document is still in existence) be proved by the production of an enlargement of a microfilm copy of that document or of the material part of it, authenticated in such manner as the court may approve.

Part VII
Microfilm copies.

72.—(1) In this Part of this Act—

"copy" and "statement" have the same meanings as in Part I of the Civil Evidence Act 1968; and

"proceedings" means criminal proceedings, including—

> (a) proceedings in the United Kingdom or elsewhere before a court-martial constituted under the Army Act 1955 or the Air Force Act 1955;
>
> (b) proceedings in the United Kingdom or elsewhere before the Courts-Martial Appeal Court—
>
>> (i) on an appeal from a court-martial so constituted or from a court-martial constituted under the Naval Discipline Act 1957; or
>>
>> (ii) on a reference under section 34 of the Courts-Martial (Appeals) Act 1968; and
>
> (c) proceedings before a Standing Civilian Court.

Part VII—supplementary.
1968 c. 64.
1955 c. 18.
1955 c. 19.
1957 c. 53.
1968 c. 20.

(2) Nothing in this Part of this Act shall prejudice any power of a court to exclude evidence (whether by preventing questions from being put or otherwise) at its discretion.

Part VIII

Evidence in Criminal Proceedings—General

Convictions and acquittals

73.—(1) Where in any proceedings the fact that a person has in the United Kingdom been convicted or acquitted of an offence otherwise than by a Service court is admissible in evidence, it may be proved by producing a certificate of conviction or, as the case may be, of acquittal relating to that offence, and proving that the person named in the certificate as having been convicted or acquitted of the offence is the person whose conviction or acquittal of the offence is to be proved.

Proof of convictions and acquittals.

(2) For the purposes of this section a certificate of conviction or of acquittal—

> (a) shall, as regards a conviction or acquittal on indictment, consist of a certificate, signed by the clerk of the court where the conviction or acquittal took place, giving the substance and effect (omitting the formal parts) of the indictment and of the conviction or acquittal; and

PART VIII

(b) shall, as regards a conviction or acquittal on a summary trial, consist of a copy of the conviction or of the dismissal of the information, signed by the clerk of the court where the conviction or acquittal took place or by the clerk of the court, if any, to which a memorandum of the conviction or acquittal was sent;

and a document purporting to be a duly signed certificate of conviction or acquittal under this section shall be taken to be such a certificate unless the contrary is proved.

(3) References in this section to the clerk of a court include references to his deputy and to any other person having the custody of the court record.

(4) The method of proving a conviction or acquittal authorised by this section shall be in addition to and not to the exclusion of any other authorised manner of proving a conviction or acquittal.

Conviction as evidence of commission of offence.

74.—(1) In any proceedings the fact that a person other than the accused has been convicted of an offence by or before any court in the United Kingdom or by a Service court outside the United Kingdom shall be admissible in evidence for the purpose of proving, where to do so is relevant to any issue in those proceedings, that that person committed that offence, whether or not any other evidence of his having committed that offence is given.

(2) In any proceedings in which by virtue of this section a person other than the accused is proved to have been convicted of an offence by or before any court in the United Kingdom or by a Service court outside the United Kingdom, he shall be taken to have committed that offence unless the contrary is proved.

(3) In any proceedings where evidence is admissible of the fact that the accused has committed an offence, in so far as that evidence is relevant to any matter in issue in the proceedings for a reason other than a tendency to show in the accused a disposition to commit the kind of offence with which he is charged, if the accused is proved to have been convicted of the offence—

(a) by or before any court in the United Kingdom; or

(b) by a Service court outside the United Kingdom,

he shall be taken to have committed that offence unless the contrary is proved.

(4) Nothing in this section shall prejudice—

(a) the admissibility in evidence of any conviction which would be admissible apart from this section; or

(b) the operation of any enactment whereby a conviction or a finding of fact in any proceedings is for the purposes of any other proceedings made conclusive evidence of any fact.

75.—(1) Where evidence that a person has been convicted of an offence is admissible by virtue of section 74 above, then without prejudice to the reception of any other admissible evidence for the purpose of identifying the facts on which the conviction was based—

(a) the contents of any document which is admissible as evidence of the conviction; and

(b) the contents of the information, complaint, indictment or charge-sheet on which the person in question was convicted,

shall be admissible in evidence for that purpose.

(2) Where in any proceedings the contents of any document are admissible in evidence by virtue of subsection (1) above, a copy of that document, or of the material part of it, purporting to be certified or otherwise authenticated by or on behalf of the court or authority having custody of that document shall be admissible in evidence and shall be taken to be a true copy of that document or part unless the contrary is shown.

(3) Nothing in any of the following—

(a) section 13 of the Powers of Criminal Courts Act 1973 (under which a conviction leading to probation or discharge is to be disregarded except as mentioned in that section);

(b) section 392 of the Criminal Procedure (Scotland) Act 1975 (which makes similar provision in respect of convictions on indictment in Scotland); and

(c) section 8 of the Probation Act (Northern Ireland) 1950 (which corresponds to section 13 of the Powers of Criminal Courts Act 1973) or any legislation which is in force in Northern Ireland for the time being and corresponds to that section,

shall affect the operation of section 74 above; and for the purposes of that section any order made by a court of summary jurisdiction in Scotland under section 182 or section 183 of the said Act of 1975 shall be treated as a conviction.

(4) Nothing in section 74 above shall be construed as rendering admissible in any proceedings evidence of any conviction other than a subsisting one.

PART VIII
Confessions.

Confessions

76.—(1) In any proceedings a confession made by an accused person may be given in evidence against him in so far as it is relevant to any matter in issue in the proceedings and is not excluded by the court in pursuance of this section.

(2) If, in any proceedings where the prosecution proposes to give in evidence a confession made by an accused person, it is represented to the court that the confession was or may have been obtained—

(a) by oppression of the person who made it; or

(b) in consequence of anything said or done which was likely, in the circumstances existing at the time, to render unreliable any confession which might be made by him in consequence thereof,

the court shall not allow the confession to be given in evidence against him except in so far as the prosecution proves to the court beyond reasonable doubt that the confession (notwithstanding that it may be true) was not obtained as aforesaid.

(3) In any proceedings where the prosecution proposes to give in evidence a confession made by an accused person, the court may of its own motion require the prosecution, as a condition of allowing it to do so, to prove that the confession was not obtained as mentioned in subsection (2) above.

(4) The fact that a confession is wholly or partly excluded in pursuance of this section shall not affect the admissibility in evidence—

(a) of any facts discovered as a result of the confession; or

(b) where the confession is relevant as showing that the accused speaks, writes or expresses himself in a particular way, of so much of the confession as is necessary to show that he does so.

(5) Evidence that a fact to which this subsection applies was discovered as a result of a statement made by an accused person shall not be admissible unless evidence of how it was discovered is given by him or on his behalf.

(6) Subsection (5) above applies—

(a) to any fact discovered as a result of a confession which is wholly excluded in pursuance of this section; and

(b) to any fact discovered as a result of a confession which is partly so excluded, if the fact is discovered as a result of the excluded part of the confession.

(7) Nothing in Part VII of this Act shall prejudice the admissibility of a confession made by an accused person.

(8) In this section "oppression" includes torture, inhuman or degrading treatment, and the use or threat of violence (whether or not amounting to torture).

77.—(1) Without prejudice to the general duty of the court at a trial on indictment to direct the jury on any matter on which it appears to the court appropriate to do so, where at such a trial—

    (a) the case against the accused depends wholly or substantially on a confession by him; and

    (b) the court is satisfied—

        (i) that he is mentally handicapped; and

        (ii) that the confession was not made in the presence of an independent person,

the court shall warn the jury that there is special need for caution before convicting the accused in reliance on the confession, and shall explain that the need arises because of the circumstances mentioned in paragraphs (a) and (b) above.

(2) In any case where at the summary trial of a person for an offence it appears to the court that a warning under subsection (1) above would be required if the trial were on indictment, the court shall treat the case as one in which there is a special need for caution before convicting the accused on his confession.

(3) In this section—

"independent person" does not include a police officer or a person employed for, or engaged on, police purposes;

"mentally handicapped", in relation to a person, means that he is in a state of arrested or incomplete development of mind which includes significant impairment of intelligence and social functioning; and

"police purposes" has the meaning assigned to it by section 64 of the Police Act 1964.

Miscellaneous

78.—(1) In any proceedings the court may refuse to allow evidence on which the prosecution proposes to rely to be given if it appears to the court that, having regard to all the circumstances, including the circumstances in which the evidence was obtained, the admission of the evidence would have such an adverse effect on the fairness of the proceedings that the court ought not to admit it.

(2) Nothing in this section shall prejudice any rule of law requiring a court to exclude evidence.

PART VIII

Time for taking accused's evidence.

79. If at the trial of any person for an offence—

(a) the defence intends to call two or more witnesses to the facts of the case; and

(b) those witnesses include the accused,

the accused shall be called before the other witness or witnesses unless the court in its discretion otherwise directs.

Competence and compellability of accused's spouse.

80.—(1) In any proceedings the wife or husband of the accused shall be competent to give evidence—

(a) subject to subsection (4) below, for the prosecution; and

(b) on behalf of the accused or any person jointly charged with the accused.

(2) In any proceedings the wife or husband of the accused shall, subject to subsection (4) below, be compellable to give evidence on behalf of the accused.

(3) In any proceedings the wife or husband of the accused shall, subject to subsection (4) below, be compellable to give evidence for the prosecution or on behalf of any person jointly charged with the accused if and only if—

(a) the offence charged involves an assault on, or injury or a threat of injury to, the wife or husband of the accused or a person who was at the material time under the age of sixteen; or

(b) the offence charged is a sexual offence alleged to have been committed in respect of a person who was at the material time under that age; or

(c) the offence charged consists of attempting or conspiring to commit, or of aiding, abetting, counselling, procuring or inciting the commission of, an offence falling within paragraph (a) or (b) above.

(4) Where a husband and wife are jointly charged with an offence neither spouse shall at the trial be competent or compellable by virtue of subsection (1)(a), (2) or (3) above to give evidence in respect of that offence unless that spouse is not, or is no longer, liable to be convicted of that offence at the trial as a result of pleading guilty or for any other reason.

(5) In any proceedings a person who has been but is no longer married to the accused shall be competent and compellable to give evidence as if that person and the accused had never been married.

(6) Where in any proceedings the age of any person at any time is material for the purposes of subsection (3) above, his age at the material time shall for the purposes of that provision be

deemed to be or to have been that which appears to the court to be or to have been his age at that time.

(7) In subsection (3)(*b*) above " sexual offence " means an offence under the Sexual Offences Act 1956, the Indecency with Children Act 1960, the Sexual Offences Act 1967, section 54 of the Criminal Law Act 1977 or the Protection of Children Act 1978.

1956 c. 69.
1960 c. 33.
1967 c. 60.
1977 c. 45.
1978 c. 37.

(8) The failure of the wife or husband of the accused to give evidence shall not be made the subject of any comment by the prosecution.

(9) Section 1(*d*) of the Criminal Evidence Act 1898 (communications between husband and wife) and section 43(1) of the Matrimonial Causes Act 1965 (evidence as to marital intercourse) shall cease to have effect.

1898 c. 36.
1965 c. 72.

81.—(1) Crown Court Rules may make provision for—

(*a*) requiring any party to proceedings before the court to disclose to the other party or parties any expert evidence which he proposes to adduce in the proceedings; and

(*b*) prohibiting a party who fails to comply in respect of any evidence with any requirement imposed by virtue of paragraph (*a*) above from adducing that evidence without the leave of the court.

Advance notice of expert evidence in Crown Court.

(2) Crown Court Rules made by virtue of this section may specify the kinds of expert evidence to which they apply and may exempt facts or matters of any description specified in the rules.

Part VIII—supplementary

82.—(1) In this Part of this Act—

" confession ", includes any statement wholly or partly adverse to the person who made it, whether made to a person in authority or not and whether made in words or otherwise ;

Part VIII—interpretation.

" court-martial " means a court-martial constituted under the Army Act 1955, the Air Force Act 1955 or the Naval Discipline Act 1957 or a disciplinary court constituted under section 50 of the said Act of 1957 ;

1955 c. 18.
1955 c. 19.
1957 c. 53.

" proceedings " means criminal proceedings, including—

(*a*) proceedings in the United Kingdom or elsewhere before a court-martial constituted under the Army Act 1955 or the Air Force Act 1955 ;

(b) proceedings in the United Kingdom or elsewhere before the Courts-Martial Appeal Court—

(i) on an appeal from a court-martial so constituted or from a court-martial constituted under the Naval Discipline Act 1957; or

(ii) on a reference under section 34 of the Courts-Martial (Appeals) Act 1968; and

(b) proceedings before a Standing Civilian Court; and

"Service court" means a court-martial or a Standing Civilian Court.

(2) In this Part of this Act references to conviction before a Service court are references—

(a) as regards a court-martial constituted under the Army Act 1955 or the Air Force Act 1955, to a finding of guilty which is, or falls to be treated as, a finding of the court duly confirmed;

(b) as regards—

(i) a court-martial; or

(ii) a disciplinary court,

constituted under the Naval Discipline Act 1957, to a finding of guilty which is, or falls to be treated as, the finding of the court;

and "convicted" shall be construed accordingly.

(3) Nothing in this Part of this Act shall prejudice any power of a court to exclude evidence (whether by preventing questions from being put or otherwise) at its discretion.

PART IX

POLICE COMPLAINTS AND DISCIPLINE

The Police Complaints Authority

83.—(1) There shall be an authority to be known as "the Police Complaints Authority" and in this Part of this Act referred to as "the Authority."

(2) Schedule 4 to this Act shall have effect in relation to the Authority.

(3) The Police Complaints Board is hereby abolished.

Handling of complaints etc.

84.—(1) Where a complaint is submitted to the chief officer of police for a police area, it shall be his duty to take any steps that appear to him to be desirable for the purpose of obtaining or preserving evidence relating to the conduct complained of.

PART IX

(2) After performing the duties imposed on him by subsection (1) above, the chief officer shall determine whether he is the appropriate authority in relation to the officer against whom the complaint was made.

(3) If he determines that he is not the appropriate authority, it shall be his duty—

(a) to send the complaint or, if it was made orally, particulars of it, to the appropriate authority; and

(b) to give notice that he has done so to the person by or on whose behalf the complaint was made.

(4) In this Part of this Act—

" complaint " means any complaint about the conduct of a police officer which is submitted—

(a) by a member of the public; or

(b) on behalf of a member of the public and with his written consent;

" the appropriate authority " means—

(a) in relation to an officer of the metropolitan police, the Commissioner of Police of the Metropolis; and

(b) in relation to an officer of any other police force—

(i) if he is a senior officer, the police authority for the force's area; and

(ii) if he is not a senior officer, the chief officer of the force;

" senior officer " means an officer holding a rank above the rank of chief superintendent.

(5) Nothing in this Part of this Act has effect in relation to a complaint in so far as it relates to the direction or control of a police force by the chief officer or the person performing the functions of the chief officer.

(6) If any conduct to which a complaint wholly or partly relates is or has been the subject of criminal or disciplinary proceedings, none of the provisions of this Part of this Act which relate to the recording and investigation of complaints have effect in relation to the complaint in so far as it relates to that conduct.

85.—(1) If a chief officer determines that he is the appropriate authority in relation to an officer about whose conduct a complaint has been made and who is not a senior officer, he shall record it.

Investigation of complaints: standard procedure.

PART IX

(2) After doing so he shall consider whether the complaint is suitable for informal resolution and may appoint an officer from his force to assist him.

(3) If it appears to the chief officer that the complaint is not suitable for informal resolution, he shall appoint an officer from his force or some other force to investigate it formally.

(4) If it appears to him that it is suitable for informal resolution, he shall seek to resolve it informally and may appoint an officer from his force to do so on his behalf.

(5) If it appears to the chief officer, after attempts have been made to resolve a complaint informally—

(a) that informal resolution of the complaint is impossible; or

(b) that the complaint is for any other reason not suitable for informal resolution,

he shall appoint an officer from his force or some other force to investigate it formally.

(6) An officer may not be appointed to investigate a complaint formally if he has previously been appointed to act in relation to it under subsection (4) above.

(7) If a chief officer requests the chief officer of some other force to provide an officer of his force for appointment under subsection (3) or (5) above, that chief officer shall provide an officer to be so appointed.

(8) No officer may be appointed under this section unless he is—

(a) of at least the rank of chief inspector; and

(b) of at least the rank of the officer against whom the complaint is made.

(9) Unless the investigation is supervised by the Authority under section 89 below, the investigating officer shall submit his report on the investigation to the chief officer.

(10) A complaint is not suitable for informal resolution unless—

(a) the member of the public concerned gives his consent; and

(b) the chief officer is satisfied that the conduct complained of, even if proved, would not justify a criminal or disciplinary charge.

Investigation of complaints against senior officers.

86.—(1) Where a complaint about the conduct of a senior officer—

(a) is submitted to the appropriate authority; or

(b) is sent to the appropriate authority under section 84(3) above,

it shall be the appropriate authority's duty to record it and, subject to subsection (2) below, to investigate it.

(2) The appropriate authority may deal with the complaint according to the appropriate authority's discretion, if satisfied that the conduct complained of, even if proved, would not justify a criminal or disciplinary charge.

(3) In any other case the appropriate authority shall appoint an officer from the appropriate authority's force or from some other force to investigate the complaint.

(4) A chief officer shall provide an officer to be appointed, if a request is made to him for one to be appointed under subsection (3) above.

(5) No officer may be appointed unless he is of at least the rank of the officer against whom the complaint is made.

(6) Unless an investigation under this section is supervised by the Authority under section 89 below, the investigating officer shall submit his report on it to the appropriate authority.

87.—(1) The appropriate authority—

(a) shall refer to the Authority—

(i) any complaint alleging that the conduct complained of resulted in the death of or serious injury to some other person; and

(ii) any complaint of a description specified for the purposes of this section in regulations made by the Secretary of State; and

(b) may refer to the Authority any complaint which is not required to be referred to them.

References of complaints to Authority.

(2) The Authority may require the submission to them for consideration of any complaint not referred to them by the appropriate authority; and it shall be the appropriate authority's duty to comply with any such requirement not later than the end of a period specified in regulations made by the Secretary of State.

(3) Where a complaint falls to be referred to the Authority under subsection (1)(a) above, it shall be the appropriate authority's duty to refer it to them not later than the end of a period specified in such regulations.

(4) In this Part of this Act "serious injury" means a fracture, damage to an internal organ, impairment of bodily function, a deep cut or a deep laceration.

PART IX
References of other matters to Authority.

88. The appropriate authority may refer to the Authority any matter which—

(a) appears to the appropriate authority to indicate that an officer may have committed a criminal offence or an offence against discipline; and

(b) is not the subject of a complaint,

if it appears to the appropriate authority that it ought to be referred by reason—

(i) of its gravity; or

(ii) of exceptional circumstances.

Supervision of investigations by Authority.

89.—(1) The Authority shall supervise the investigation—

(a) of any complaint alleging that the conduct of a police officer resulted in the death of or serious injury to some other person; and

(b) of any other description of complaint specified for the purposes of this section in regulations made by the Secretary of State.

(2) The Authority shall supervise the investigation—

(a) of any complaint the investigation of which they are not required to supervise under subsection (1) above; and

(b) of any matter referred to them under section 88 above,

if they consider that it is desirable in the public interest that they should supervise that investigation.

(3) Where the Authority have made a determination under this section, it shall be their duty to notify it to the appropriate authority.

(4) Where an investigation is to be supervised by the Authority they may require—

(a) that no appointment shall be made under section 85(3) or 86(3) above unless they have given notice to the appropriate authority that they approve the officer whom that authority propose to appoint; or

(b) if such an appointment has already been made and the Authority are not satisfied with the officer appointed, that—

(i) the appropriate authority shall, as soon as is reasonably practicable, select another officer and notify the Authority that they propose to appoint him; and

(ii) the appointment shall not be made unless the Authority give notice to the appropriate authority that they approve that officer.

(5) It shall be the duty of the Secretary of State by regulations to provide that the Authority shall have power, subject to any restrictions or conditions specified in the regulations, to impose requirements as to a particular investigation additional to any requirements imposed by virtue of subsection (4) above; and it shall be the duty of a police officer to comply with any requirement imposed on him by virtue of the regulations.

(6) At the end of an investigation which the Authority have supervised the investigating officer—

(a) shall submit a report on the investigation to the Authority; and

(b) shall send a copy to the appropriate authority.

(7) After considering a report submitted to them under subsection (6) above, the Authority shall submit an appropriate statement to the appropriate authority.

(8) If it is practicable to do so, the Authority, when submitting the appropriate statement under subsection (7) above, shall send a copy to the officer whose conduct has been investigated.

(9) If—

(a) the investigation related to a complaint; and

(b) it is practicable to do so,

the Authority shall also send a copy of the appropriate statement to the person by or on behalf of whom the complaint was made.

(10) In subsection (7) above "appropriate statement" means a statement—

(a) whether the investigation was or was not conducted to the Authority's satisfaction;

(b) specifying any respect in which it was not so conducted; and

(c) dealing with any such other matters as the Secretary of State may by regulations provide.

(11) The power to issue an appropriate statement includes power to issue separate statements in respect of the disciplinary and criminal aspects of an investigation.

(12) No disciplinary charge shall be brought before the appropriate statement is submitted to the appropriate authority.

(13) Subject to subsection (14) below, neither the appropriate authority nor the Director of Public Prosecutions shall bring criminal proceedings before the appropriate statement is submitted to the appropriate authority.

(14) The restriction imposed by subsection (13) above does not apply if it appears to the Director that there are exceptional

PART IX circumstances which make it undesirable to wait for the submission of the appropriate statement.

Steps to be taken after investigation—general.

90.—(1) It shall be the duty of the appropriate authority, on receiving—

(a) a report concerning the conduct of a senior officer which is submitted to them under section 86(6) above ; or

(b) a copy of a report concerning the conduct of a senior officer which is sent to them under section 89(6) above,

to send a copy of the report to the Director of Public Prosecutions unless the report satisfies them that no criminal offence has been committed.

(2) Nothing in the following provisions of this section or in sections 91 to 94 below has effect in relation to senior officers.

(3) On receiving—

(a) a report concerning the conduct of an officer who is not a senior officer which is submitted to him under section 85(9) above ; or

(b) a copy of a report concerning the conduct of such an officer which is sent to him under section 89(6) above

it shall be the duty of a chief officer of police—

(i) to determine whether the report indicates that a criminal offence may have been committed by a member of the police force for his area ; and

(ii) if he determines that it does, to consider whether the offence indicated is such that the officer ought to be charged with it.

(4) If the chief officer—

(a) determines that the report does indicate that a criminal offence may have been committed by a member of the police force for his area ; and

(b) considers that the offence indicated is such that the officer ought to be charged with it,

he shall send a copy of the report to the Director of Public Prosecutions.

(5) Subject to section 91(1) below, after the Director has dealt with the question of criminal proceedings, the chief officer shall send the Authority a memorandum, signed by him and stating whether he has preferred disciplinary charges in respect of the conduct which was the subject of the investigation and, if not, his reasons for not doing so.

(6) If the chief officer—
- (a) determines that the report does indicate that a criminal offence may have been committed by a member of the police force for his area; and
- (b) considers that the offence indicated is not such that the officer ought to be charged with it,

he shall send the Authority a memorandum to that effect, signed by him and stating whether he proposes to prefer disciplinary charges in respect of the conduct which was the subject of the investigation and, if not, his reasons for not proposing to do so.

(7) Subject to section 91(1) below, if the chief officer considers that the report does not indicate that a criminal offence may have been committed by a member of the police force for his area, he shall send the Authority a memorandum to that effect, signed by him and stating whether he has preferred disciplinary charges in respect of the conduct which was the subject of the investigation and, if not, his reasons for not doing so.

(8) A memorandum under this section—
- (a) shall give particulars—
  - (i) of any disciplinary charges which a chief officer has preferred or proposes to prefer in respect of the conduct which was the subject of the investigation; and
  - (ii) of any exceptional circumstances affecting the case by reason of which he considers that section 94 below should apply to the hearing; and
- (b) shall state his opinion of the complaint or other matter to which it relates.

(9) Where the investigation—
- (a) related to conduct which was the subject of a complaint; and
- (b) was not supervised by the Authority,

the chief officer shall send the Authority—
- (i) a copy of the complaint or of the record of the complaint; and
- (ii) a copy of the report of the investigation.

at the same time as he sends them the memorandum.

(10) Subject to section 93(6) below—
- (a) if a chief officer's memorandum states that he proposes to prefer disciplinary charges, it shall be his duty to prefer and proceed with them; and
- (b) if such a memorandum states that he has preferred such charges, it shall be his duty to proceed with them.

PART IX

Steps to be taken where accused has admitted charges.

91.—(1) No memorandum need be sent to the Authority under section 90 above if disciplinary charges have been preferred in respect of the conduct which was the subject of the investigation and the accused has admitted the charges and has not withdrawn his admission.

(2) In any such case the chief officer shall send to the Authority, after the conclusion of the disciplinary proceedings (including any appeal to the Secretary of State), particulars of the disciplinary charges preferred and of any punishment imposed.

(3) If—

(a) the charges related to conduct which was the subject of a complaint; and

(b) the investigation of the complaint was not supervised by the Authority,

the chief officer shall also send the Authority—

(i) a copy of the complaint or of the record of the complaint; and

(ii) a copy of the report of the investigation.

Powers of Authority to direct reference of reports etc. to Director of Public Prosecutions.

92.—(1) When a chief officer of police has performed all duties imposed on him by sections 90 and 91 above in relation to the report of an investigation concerning the conduct of an officer who is not a senior officer, it shall be the duty of the Authority—

(a) to determine whether the report indicates that a criminal offence may have been committed by that officer; and

(b) if so, to consider whether the offence is such that the officer ought to be charged with it.

(2) If the Authority consider that the officer ought to be charged, it shall be their duty to direct the chief officer to send the Director of Public Prosecutions a copy of the report.

(3) When the Authority give a direction under subsection (2) above, they may also direct the chief officer to send the Director the information contained in the memorandum under section 90 above.

(4) If the investigation was an investigation of a complaint, the Authority shall direct the chief officer to send the Director a copy of the complaint or of the record of the complaint.

(5) It shall be the duty of a chief officer to comply with any direction under this section.

(6) Sections 90 and 91 above shall apply where a copy of a report is sent to the Director under this section as they apply where a copy is sent to him under section 90(4) above.

93.—(1) Where a memorandum under section 90 above states that a chief officer of police has not preferred disciplinary charges or does not propose to do so, the Authority may recommend him to prefer such disciplinary charges as they may specify.

Powers of Authority as to disciplinary charges.

(2) Subject to subsection (6) below, a chief officer may not withdraw charges which he has preferred in accordance with a recommendation under subsection (1) above.

(3) If after the Authority have made a recommendation under this section and consulted the chief officer he is still unwilling to prefer such charges as the Authority consider appropriate, they may direct him to prefer such charges as they may specify.

(4) Where the Authority give a chief officer a direction under this section, they shall furnish him with a written statement of their reasons for doing so.

(5) Subject to subsection (6) below, it shall be the duty of a chief officer to prefer and proceed with charges specified in such a direction.

(6) The Authority may give a chief officer leave—

    (a) not to prefer charges which section 90(10) above or subsection (5) above would otherwise oblige him to prefer; or

    (b) not to proceed with charges with which section 90(10) above or subsection (2) or (5) above would otherwise oblige him to proceed.

(7) The Authority may request a chief officer of police to furnish them with such information as they may reasonably require for the purpose of discharging their functions under this section.

(8) It shall be the duty of a chief officer to comply with any such request.

94.—(1) Where a chief officer of police prefers a disciplinary charge in respect of a matter to which a memorandum under section 90 above relates, this section applies—

Disciplinary tribunals.

    (a) to the hearing of any charge in pursuance of a direction under section 93 above; and

    (b) to the hearing of any other charge to which the Authority direct that it shall apply.

(2) The Authority may direct that this section shall apply to the hearing of a charge if they consider that to be desirable by reason of any exceptional circumstances affecting the case.

PART IX

(3) Where this section applies to the hearing of a disciplinary charge—

(a) the function of determining whether the accused is guilty of the charge shall be discharged by a tribunal consisting of—

(i) a chairman who shall, subject to subsection (4) below, be the chief officer of police by whom that function would fall to be discharged apart from this section; and

(ii) two members of the Authority nominated by the Authority, being members who have not been concerned with the case; and

(b) the function of determining any punishment to be imposed shall, subject to subsection (7) below, be discharged by the chairman after consulting the other members of the tribunal.

(4) Where—

(a) the accused is a member of the metropolitan police force; and

(b) the function of determining whether he is guilty of the charge would, apart from this section, fall to be discharged by a person or persons other than a chief officer of police (whether the Commissioner of Police of the Metropolis or the chief officer of another police force),

the chairman of the tribunal shall be—

(i) a person nominated by the Commissioner, being either an Assistant Commissioner of Police of the Metropolis or an officer of the metropolitan police force of such rank as may be prescribed by regulations made by the Secretary of State; or

(ii) in default of any such nomination, the Commissioner.

(5) The Secretary of State may by regulations provide for the procedure to be followed by tribunals constituted under this section.

(6) The decision of the tribunal as to whether the accused is guilty of the charge may be a majority decision.

(7) Where—

(a) the chairman of the tribunal is not the chief officer of police of the police force to which the accused belongs; and

(b) that chief officer is neither interested in the case otherwise than in his capacity as such nor a material witness, the function of determining any punishment to be imposed shall be discharged by that chief officer after considering any recommendation as to punishment made by the chairman.

(8) Before making any recommendation the chairman shall consult the other members of the tribunal.

(9) Where—
  (a) this section applies to the hearing of a disciplinary charge; and
  (b) there is another disciplinary charge against the accused which, in the opinion of the chief officer of police of the police force to which he belongs, can conveniently and fairly be determined at the same time,

the chief officer may direct that this section shall apply also to the hearing of the other charge.

95. Every police authority in carrying out their duty with respect to the maintenance of an adequate and efficient police force, and inspectors of constabulary in carrying out their duties with respect to the efficiency of any police force, shall keep themselves informed as to the working of sections 84 to 93 above in relation to the force. *(Information as to the manner of dealing with complaints etc.)*

96.—(1) An agreement for the establishment in relation to any body of constables maintained by an authority other than a police authority of procedures corresponding to any of those established by or by virtue of this Part of this Act may, with the approval of the Secretary of State, be made between the Authority and the authority maintaining the body of constables. *(Constabularies maintained by authorities other than police authorities.)*

(2) Where no such procedures are in force in relation to any body of constables, the Secretary of State may by order establish such procedures.

(3) An agreement under this section may at any time be varied or terminated with the approval of the Secretary of State.

(4) Before making an order under this section the Secretary of State shall consult—
  (a) the Authority; and
  (b) the authority maintaining the body of constables to whom the order would relate.

(5) The power to make orders under this section shall be exercisable by statutory instrument; and any statutory instrument containing such an order shall be subject to annulment in pursuance of a resolution of either House of Parliament.

PART IX

(6) Nothing in any other enactment shall prevent an authority who maintain a body of constables from carrying into effect procedures established by virtue of this section.

(7) No such procedures shall have effect in relation to anything done by a constable outside England and Wales.

Reports.

97.—(1) The Authority shall, at the request of the Secretary of State, report to him on such matters relating generally to their functions as the Secretary of State may specify, and the Authority may for that purpose carry out research into any such matters.

(2) The Authority may make a report to the Secretary of State on any matters coming to their notice under this Part of this Act to which they consider that his attention should be drawn by reason of their gravity or of other exceptional circumstances; and the Authority shall send a copy of any such report to the police authority and to the chief officer of police of any police force which appears to the Authority to be concerned or, if the report concerns any such body of constables as is mentioned in section 96 above, to the authority maintaining it and the officer having the direction and the control of it.

(3) As soon as practicable after the end of each calendar year the Authority shall make to the Secretary of State a report on the discharge of their functions during that year.

(4) The Authority shall keep under review the working of sections 84 to 96 above and shall make to the Secretary of State a report on it at least once in every three years after the coming into force of this section.

(5) The Secretary of State shall lay before Parliament a copy of every report received by him under this section and shall cause every such report to be published.

(6) The Authority shall send to every police authority—
  (a) a copy of every report made by the Authority under subsection (3) above; and
  (b) any statistical or other general information which relates to the year dealt with by the report and to the area of that authority and which the Authority consider should be brought to the police authority's attention in connection with their functions under section 95 above.

Restriction on disclosure of information.

98.—(1) No information received by the Authority in connection with any of their functions under sections 84 to 97 above or regulations made by virtue of section 99 below shall be disclosed by any person who is or has been a member, officer or servant of the Authority except—

(a) to the Secretary of State or to a member, officer or servant of the Authority or, so far as may be necessary for the proper discharge of the functions of the Authority, to other persons;

(b) for the purposes of any criminal, civil or disciplinary proceedings; or

(c) in the form of a summary or other general statement made by the Authority which does not identify the person from whom the information was received or any person to whom it relates.

(2) Any person who discloses information in contravention of this section shall be guilty of an offence and liable on summary conviction to a fine of an amount not exceeding level 5 on the standard scale, as defined in section 75 of the Criminal Justice Act 1982.

99.—(1) The Secretary of State may make regulations as to the procedure to be followed under this Part of this Act.

(2) It shall be the duty of the Secretary of State to provide by regulations—

(a) that, subject to such exceptions as may be specified by the regulations, a chief officer of police shall furnish, in accordance with such procedure as may be so specified, a copy of, or of the record of, a complaint against a member of the police force for his area—

(i) to the person by or on behalf of whom the complaint was made; and

(ii) to the officer against whom it was made;

(b) procedures for the informal resolution of complaints of such descriptions as may be specified in the regulations, and for giving the person who made the complaint a record of the outcome of any such procedure if he applies for one within such period as the regulations may provide;

(c) procedures for giving a police officer against whom a complaint is made which falls to be resolved informally an opportunity to comment orally or in writing on the complaint;

(d) for cases in which any provision of this Part of this Act is not to apply where a complaint, other than a complaint which falls to be resolved by an informal procedure, is withdrawn or the complainant indicates that he does not wish any further steps to be taken;

PART IX

(e) for enabling the Authority to dispense with any requirement of this Part of this Act;

(f) procedures for the reference or submission of complaints or other matters to the Authority;

(g) for the time within which the Authority are to give a notification under section 89(3) above;

(h) that the Authority shall be supplied with such information or documents of such description as may be specified in the regulations at such time or in such circumstances as may be so specified;

(j) that any action or decision of the Authority which they take in consequence of their receipt of a memorandum under section 90 above shall be notified if it is an action or decision of a description specified in the regulations, to the person concerned and that, in connection with such a notification, the Authority shall have power to furnish him with any relevant information;

(k) that chief officers of police shall have power to delegate any functions conferred on them by or by virtue of the foregoing provisions of this Part of this Act, other than their functions under section 94(3) above.

Regulations—supplementary.

100.—(1) Regulations under this Part of this Act may make different provision for different circumstances and may authorise the Secretary of State to make provision for any purposes specified in the regulations.

(2) Before making regulations under this Part of this Act, the Secretary of State shall furnish a draft of the regulations to the Police Advisory Board for England and Wales and take into consideration any representations made by that Board.

(3) Any power to make regulations under this Part of this Act shall be exercisable by statutory instrument.

(4) Subject to subsection (5) below, regulations under this Part of this Act shall be subject to annulment in pursuance of a resolution of either House of Parliament.

(5) Regulations to which this subsection applies shall not be made unless a draft of them has been approved by resolution of each House of Parliament.

(6) Subsection (5) above applies to regulations made by virtue—

(a) of section 87(1)(a)(ii) or 89(1)(b) or (5) above;

(b) of section 99(2)(b) or (e) above.

Amendments of discipline provisions

101.—(1) Regulations under section 33(2)(*e*) of the Police Act 1964 (discipline regulations) shall provide—

>Discipline regulations 1964 c. 48.

(*a*) for the determination of questions whether offences against discipline have been committed;

(*b*) for racially discriminatory behaviour to be made a specific disciplinary offence; and

(*c*) for members of police forces who are found to have committed such offences to be punished by way of dismissal, requirement to resign, reduction in rank, reduction in rate of pay, fine, reprimand or caution.

(2) In the case of a police force maintained under section 1 of that Act (county or combined police force) the regulations shall provide for the functions mentioned in subsection (1)(*a*) or (*c*) above to be discharged—

(*a*) in relation to the chief constable, any deputy chief constable and any assistant chief constable, by the police authority;

(*b*) in relation to any other member of the police force, by the chief constable,

but subject, in a case within paragraph (*b*) of this subsection, to section 94 above and the following provisions of this section.

(3) The regulations shall provide for the functions mentioned in subsection (1)(*a*) and (*c*) above to be discharged by another chief officer of police if, in a case within subsection (2)(*b*) above, the chief constable—

(*a*) is interested in the case otherwise than in his capacity as such; or

(*b*) is a material witness.

(4) Without prejudice to subsection (3) above, the regulations may, as respects any case within subsection (2) (*b*) above, provide—

(*a*) for enabling a chief constable, where he considers it appropriate to do so, to direct that his function under subsection (1)(*a*) above shall be discharged by another chief officer of police; and

(*b*) where such a direction is given, for the function mentioned in subsection (1)(*c*) above to be discharged by the chief constable after considering any recommendation as to punishment made by the other chief officer of police.

(5) Subject to subsection (6) below, the regulations may provide for enabling a chief constable to direct that his functions under

PART IX

subsection (1) above may be discharged by a deputy chief constable in any case—

(a) which is within subsection (2)(b) above;

(b) in which the decision that a disciplinary charge is to be brought is taken, in accordance with the regulations, by an assistant chief constable; and

(c) in which it appears appropriate to the chief constable so to direct.

(6) In subsection (5) above the reference to functions under subsection (1) above does not include the functions mentioned in section 94(3) above.

(7) If regulations provide by virtue of subsection (5) above that any of the functions of a chief constable may be discharged by a deputy chief constable, they may provide that the deputy chief constable shall have power or shall be under a duty to remit any matter to the chief constable in such circumstances as the regulations may specify.

(8) If regulations provide as mentioned in subsection (5) above, they shall also provide—

(a) that a deputy chief constable shall have power to punish only by way of reduction in rate of pay, fine, reprimand or caution;

(b) that a police officer dealt with by a deputy chief constable may appeal to the chief constable; and

(c) that on such an appeal the chief constable shall have no power to award a punishment greater than the punishment awarded by the deputy chief constable.

1964 c. 48.

(9) Subsections (2) to (8) above shall apply in the case of the City of London police force as they apply in the case of a police force maintained under section 1 of the Police Act 1964 but with the substitution—

(a) subject to paragraph (b) below, for references to a deputy chief constable or an assistant chief constable of references to an assistant commissioner of police for the City of London and any officer holding a rank appearing to the Secretary of State to correspond to that of assistant chief constable in a force maintained under that section;

(b) for the reference in subsection (5) to a deputy chief constable of a reference to an officer of the City of London police force holding a rank such as is mentioned in paragraph (a) above but who is not the officer who has taken the decision mentioned in paragraph (b) of that subsection; and

(c) for references to the chief constable of references to the Commissioner of Police for the City of London.

102.—(1) On the hearing of a disciplinary charge against a police officer of the rank of chief superintendent or below the punishment of dismissal, requirement to resign or reduction in rank may not be awarded unless he has been given an opportunity to elect to be legally represented at the hearing.

Representation at disciplinary proceedings.

(2) Where such an officer so elects, he may be represented at the hearing, at his option, either by counsel or by a solicitor.

(3) Except in a case where such an officer has been given an opportunity to elect to be legally represented and has so elected, he may only be represented at the hearing of a disciplinary charge by another member of a police force.

(4) Regulations under section 33(2)(e) of the Police Act 1964 shall specify—

(a) a procedure for notifying an officer of the effect of subsections (1) to (3) above;

(b) when he is to be so notified and when he is to give notice whether or not he wishes to be legally represented at the hearing.

1964 c. 48.

(5) If an officer—

(a) fails without reasonable cause to give notice in accordance with the regulations that he wishes to be legally represented; or

(b) gives notice in accordance with the regulations that he does not wish to be legally represented,

any such punishment as is mentioned in subsection (1) above may be awarded without his being legally represented.

(6) If an officer has given notice in accordance with the regulations that he wishes to be legally represented, the case against him may be presented by counsel or a solicitor whether or not he is actually so represented.

103.—(1) The following section shall be substituted for section 37 of the Police Act 1964—

Disciplinary appeals.

" *Disciplinary appeals to Secretary of State.*

37.—(1) A member of a police force who is dealt with for an offence against discipline may appeal to the Secretary of State—

(a) against the decision on the disciplinary charge which was preferred against him;

(b) against any punishment awarded,

except where he has a right of appeal to some other person; and in that case he may appeal to the Secretary of State from any decision of that other person.

(2) On an appeal the Secretary of State may make an order allowing or dismissing the appeal.

(3) Subject to subsection (4) below, in any case where it appears to him that it is appropriate to do so, he may substitute some other punishment.

(4) The Secretary of State may not substitute another punishment unless it appears to him—

- (a) that the person or tribunal who heard the disciplinary charge could have awarded it; and
- (b) that it is less severe than the punishment awarded by that person or tribunal.

(5) The Secretary of State may direct an appellant to pay the whole or any part of his own costs; but, subject to any such direction, all the costs and expenses of an appeal under this section, including the costs of the parties, shall be defrayed out of the police fund.

(6) Schedule 5 to this Act shall have effect in relation to any appeal under this section.".

(2) The following Schedule shall be substituted for Schedule 5 to that Act—

"Section 37.

SCHEDULE 5

DISCIPLINARY APPEALS

Notice of appeal

1. Any appeal under section 37 of this Act (in this Schedule referred to as 'the principal section') shall be instituted by giving a notice of appeal within the time prescribed under this Schedule.

Respondent

2.—(1) On any appeal under the principal section against the decision of a police authority the respondent shall be that authority.

(2) On any other appeal under that section the respondent shall be the chief officer of police of the police force to which the appellant belongs or such other person as the Secretary of State may direct; and the Secretary of State may direct any respondent under this sub-paragraph to act in relation to the

appeal in consultation with such other person or persons as the Secretary of State may specify.

Inquiries

3.—(1) The Secretary of State may appoint three persons to hold an inquiry into and report to him on any appeal under the principal section other than an appeal from a decision of a police authority and, subject to sub-paragraph (2) below, shall do so where—

(a) it appears to him that the appeal cannot be properly determined without taking evidence; or

(b) the appellant has been punished by way of dismissal, requirement to resign or reduction in rank and has requested that such persons be appointed.

(2) The Secretary of State need not make an appointment under sub-paragraph (1) above if he is satisfied that there are sufficient grounds for allowing the appeal without an inquiry.

(3) The persons appointed under sub-paragraph (1) above shall be—

(a) a barrister or solicitor, who shall be chairman;

(b) a serving or retired inspector of constabulary or a retired chief officer; and

(c) a retired officer of appropriate rank within the meaning of sub-paragraph (4) below.

(4) A retired officer of appropriate rank means—

(a) where the appellant was, immediately before the disciplinary proceedings, of the rank of chief superintendent or superintendent, a retired police officer who at the time of his retirement was of either of those ranks; and

(b) in any other case, a retired police officer who at the time of his retirement was of the rank of chief inspector or below.

(5) The Secretary of State may appoint one or more persons to hold an inquiry into and report to him on an appeal under the principal section from a decision of a police authority.

(6) The Secretary of State may require persons appointed under this paragraph to deal in their report with any particular matter specified by him.

(7) Subsections (2) and (3) of section 250 of the Local Government Act 1972 shall apply to any inquiry under this paragraph as they apply to an inquiry under that section.

(8) The Secretary of State may require persons appointed under this paragraph to hold a hearing.

(9) Persons so appointed shall hold a hearing in any case where they are not required to do so under sub-paragraph (8) above, unless it appears to them that it is unnecessary to do so.

(10) A decision whether to hold a hearing shall not be taken under sub-paragraph (9) above unless both the appellant and the respondent have been afforded an opportunity to make written or, if either so requests, oral representations and any such representations have been considered.

(11) Where a hearing is held in the course of an inquiry, the appellant shall have the right to appear by a serving member of a police force or by counsel or a solicitor; and the respondent shall have the right to appear by an officer of the police force or by the clerk or other officer of the police authority or by counsel or a solicitor.

(12) Before making an order under the principal section the Secretary of State shall consider any report made to him under this paragraph, as well as the notice of appeal and any other documents submitted to him by the appellant and the respondent in accordance with rules under this Schedule.

(13) The Secretary of State may, before making an order under the principal section, remit the case for further investigation by the person or persons who held the inquiry or, if he thinks fit, for further consideration by the person or persons whose decision is the subject of the appeal.

Notice and effect of orders

4.—(1) A copy of any order made by the Secretary of State, together with a written statement of his reasons for making it, shall as soon as made be sent to the appellant and the respondent together with, if an inquiry was held, a copy of the report of the person or persons who held the inquiry; and the order shall be final and binding upon all parties.

(2) Where an appeal is allowed or the punishment is varied by the Secretary of State, the order shall take effect by way of substitution for the decision appealed from, and as from the date of that decision; and where the effect of the order is to reinstate the appellant in the force or in his rank, he shall, for the purpose of reckoning service for pension, and, to such extent (if any) as may be determined by the order, for the purpose of pay, be deemed to have served in the force or in that rank, as the case may be, continuously from the date of the decision to the date of his reinstatement and, if he were suspended for a period immediately preceding the date of the decision, the order shall deal with the suspension.

(3) Any costs payable under the principal section shall be subject to taxation in such manner as the Secretary of State may direct.

Rules

5.—(1) The Secretary of State may make rules as to the procedure on appeals and at inquiries under this Schedule and in particular, but without prejudice to the generality of this provision, may make rules—

- (a) prescribing the form and content of the notice of appeal and the documents to be submitted by the appellant and the time within which such documents are to be submitted; and
- (b) prescribing the documents to be submitted and the time within which they are to be submitted by the respondent; and
- (c) providing for the person or persons holding an inquiry to receive evidence or representations in writing instead of holding a hearing.

(2) Any rules made under this paragraph shall be laid before Parliament after being made.".

General

104.—(1) Where a member of a police force has been convicted or acquitted of a criminal offence he shall not be liable to be charged with any offence against discipline which is in substance the same as the offence of which he has been convicted or acquitted.

Restrictions on subsequent proceedings.

PART IX

(2) Subsection (1) above shall not be construed as applying to a charge in respect of an offence against discipline which consists in having been found guilty of a criminal offence.

(3) Subject to subsection (4) below, no statement made by any person for the purpose of the informal resolution of a complaint shall be admissible in any subsequent criminal, civil or disciplinary proceedings.

(4) A statement is not rendered inadmissible by subsection (3) above if it consists of or includes an admission relating to a matter which does not fall to be resolved informally.

Guidelines concerning discipline, complaints etc.

105.—(1) The Secretary of State may issue guidance to chief officers of police and to other police officers concerning the discharge of their functions—

(*a*) under this Part of this Act; and

(*b*) otherwise in connection with discipline;

and police officers shall have regard to any such guidance in the discharge of their functions.

(2) Guidance may not be issued under subsection (1) above in relation to the handling of a particular case.

(3) A failure on the part of a police officer to have regard to any guidance issued under subsection (1) above when determining—

(*a*) whether an officer has committed an offence against discipline; or

(*b*) the punishment to be awarded for such an offence,

shall be admissible in evidence on any appeal from the determination.

(4) In discharging their functions under section 93 above the Authority shall have regard to any guidance given to them by the Secretary of State with respect to such matters affecting the preferring and withdrawing of disciplinary charges as are for the time being the subject of guidance under subsection (1) above, and shall have regard in particular, but without prejudice to the generality of this subsection, to any such guidance as to the principles to be applied in cases that involve any question of criminal proceedings and are not governed by section 104 above.

(5) The report of the Authority under section 97(3) above shall contain a statement of any guidance given to the Authority under subsection (4) above during the year to which the report relates.

Part X

Police—General

106.—(1) Arrangements shall be made in each police area for obtaining the views of people in that area about matters concerning the policing of the area and for obtaining their co-operation with the police in preventing crime in the area.

Arrangements for obtaining the views of the community on policing.

(2) Except as provided by subsections (3) to (7) below, arrangements for each police area shall be made by the police authority after consulting the chief constable as to the arrangements that would be appropriate.

(3) The Secretary of State shall issue guidance to the Commissioner of Police of the Metropolis concerning arrangements for the Metropolitan Police District; and the Commissioner shall make such arrangements after taking account of that guidance.

(4) The Commissioner shall make separate arrangements—
  (a) for each London borough;
  (b) for each district which falls wholly within the Metropolitan Police District; and
  (c) for each part of a district which falls partly within that District.

(5) The Commissioner shall consult the council of each London borough as to the arrangements that would be appropriate for the borough.

(6) The Commissioner shall consult the council of each such district as is mentioned in subsection (4)(b) above as to the arrangements that would be appropriate for the district.

(7) The Commissioner shall consult the council of each such district as is mentioned in subsection (4)(c) above as to the arrangements that would be appropriate for the part of the district for which it falls to him to make arrangements.

(8) The Common Council of the City of London shall issue guidance to the Commissioner of Police for the City of London concerning arrangements for the City; and the Commissioner shall make such arrangements after taking account of that guidance.

(9) A body or person whose duty it is to make arrangements under this section shall review the arrangements so made from time to time.

(10) If it appears to the Secretary of State that arrangements in a police area are not adequate for the purposes set out in subsection (1) above, he may require the body or person whose duty it is to make arrangements in that area to submit a report to him concerning the arrangements.

(11) After considering the report the Secretary of State may require the body or person who submitted it to review the arrangements and submit a further report to him concerning them.

(12) A body or person whose duty it is to make arrangements shall be under the same duties to consult when reviewing arrangements as when making them.

Police officers performing duties of higher rank.

107.—(1) For the purpose of any provision of this Act or any other Act under which a power in respect of the investigation of offences or the treatment of persons in police custody is exercisable only by or with the authority of a police officer of at least the rank of superintendent, an officer of the rank of chief inspector shall be treated as holding the rank of superintendent if he has been authorised by an officer of at least the rank of chief superintendent to exercise the power or, as the case may be, to give his authority for its exercise.

(2) For the purpose of any provision of this Act or any other Act under which such a power is exercisable only by or with the authority of an officer of at least the rank of inspector, an officer of the rank of sergeant shall be treated as holding the rank of inspector if he has been authorised by an officer of at least the rank of chief superintendent to exercise the power or, as the case may be, to give his authority for its exercise.

Deputy chief constables.

108.—(1) The office of deputy chief constable is hereby abolished.

1964 c. 48.

(2) In section 6 of the Police Act 1964—

  (a) in subsection (1), after the word "a" there shall be inserted the words "person holding the rank of"; and

  (b) in subsection (4), for the words from the beginning to "of", in the second place where it occurs, there shall be substituted the words "Appointments or promotions to the rank of deputy chief constable or".

(3) The following section shall be inserted after that section—

"Deputy chief constables—supplementary.

6A.—(1) Any police force maintained under section 1 of this Act may include more than one person holding the rank of deputy chief constable, but only if the additional person or persons holding that rank—

(a) was a deputy chief constable before a period—
   (i) of central service ; or
   (ii) of overseas service, as defined in section 3 of the Police (Overseas Service) Act 1945 ; or
   (iii) of service in pursuance of an appointment under section 10 of the Overseas Development and Co-operation Act 1980 as an officer to whom that section applied ; or
(b) became a deputy chief constable by virtue of section 58(2) of this Act.

(2) If there is more than one person who holds the rank of deputy chief constable in a police force maintained under section 1 of this Act, one of the persons who hold it shall be designated as the officer having the powers and duties conferred on a deputy chief constable by section 6(1) of this Act.

(3) A person shall be designated under subsection (2) of this section by the police authority after consultation with the chief constable and subject to the approval of the Secretary of State.".

(4) In section 5 of the Police (Scotland) Act 1967—
(a) in subsection (1), after the word " a " there shall be inserted the words " person holding the rank of " ;
(b) subsection (3) shall be omitted ; and
(c) in subsection (5), for the words from the beginning to " of ", in the second place where it occurs, there shall be substituted the words " Appointments or promotions to the rank of deputy chief constable or ".

(5) The following section shall be inserted after that section—

"Deputy chief constables— supplementary.

5A.—(1) Any police force may include more than one person holding the rank of deputy chief constable, but only if the additional person or persons holding that rank—
(a) was a deputy chief constable before a period—
   (i) of central service ; or
   (ii) of overseas service, as defined in section 3 of the Police (Overseas Service) Act 1945 ; or
   (iii) of service in pursuance of an appointment under section 10 of the Over-

PART X

seas Development and Co-operation Act 1980 as an officer to whom that section applied; or

(b) became a deputy chief constable by virtue of section 23(2) of this Act.

(2) If there is more than one person in a police force who holds the rank of deputy chief constable, one of the persons who hold it shall be designated as the officer having the powers and duties conferred on a deputy chief constable by section 5(1) of this Act.

(3) A person shall be designated under subsection (2) of this section by the police authority after consultation with the chief constable and subject to the approval of the Secretary of State.".

1964 c. 48.
1967 c. 77.

(6) In section 58(2) of the Police Act 1964 and section 23(2) of the Police (Scotland) Act 1967 (under both of which a chief constable affected by an amalgamation holds the rank of assistant chief constable) for the word "assistant" there shall be substituted the word "deputy".

Amendments relating to Police Federations.

109. In section 44 of the Police Act 1964—

(a) in subsection (1), for the word "and", in the last place where it occurs, there shall be substituted the words "affecting individuals, except as provided by subsection (1A) below, and questions of";

(b) the following subsections shall be inserted after that subsection—

"(1A) A Police Federation may represent a member of a police force at any disciplinary proceedings or on an appeal from any such proceedings.

(1B) Except on an appeal to the Secretary of State or as provided by section 102 of the Police and Criminal Evidence Act 1984, a member of a police force may only be represented under subsection (1A) above by another member of a police force."; and

(c) in subsection (3), after the word "Federations", in the first place where it occurs, there shall be inserted the words "or authorise the Federations to make rules concerning such matters relating to their constitution and proceedings as may be specified in the regulations.".

Functions of special constables in Scotland.

110. Subsection (6) of section 17 of the Police (Scotland) Act 1967 (restriction on functions of special constables) is hereby repealed.

111.—(1) In section 26 to the Police (Scotland) Act 1967 (regulations as to government and administration of police forces)—

(a) after subsection (1) there shall be inserted the following subsection—

"(1A) Regulations under this section may authorise the Secretary of State, the police authority or the chief constable to make provision for any purpose specified in the regulations."; and

(b) at the end there shall be inserted the following subsection—

"(10) Any statutory instrument made under this section shall be subject to annulment in pursuance of a resolution of either House of Parliament.".

Part X — Regulations for Police Forces and Police Cadets—Scotland. 1967 c. 77.

(2) In section 27 of the said Act of 1967 (regulations for police cadets) in subsection (3) for the word "(9)" there shall be substituted the words "(1A), (9) and (10)".

112.—(1) An officer belonging to the metropolitan police force who is assigned to the protection of any person or property in Scotland shall in the discharge of that duty have the powers and privileges of a constable of a police force maintained under the Police (Scotland) Act 1967.

Metropolitan police officers.

(2) An officer belonging to the metropolitan police force who is assigned to the protection of any person or property in Northern Ireland shall in the discharge of that duty have the powers and privileges of a constable of the Royal Ulster Constabulary.

Part XI

Miscellaneous and Supplementary

113.—(1) The Secretary of State may by order direct that any provision of this Act which relates to investigations of offences conducted by police officers or to persons detained by the police shall apply, subject to such modifications as he may specify, to investigations of offences conducted under the Army Act 1955, the Air Force Act 1955 or the Naval Discipline Act 1957. or to persons under arrest under any of those Acts.

Application of Act to Armed Forces. 1955 c. 18. 1955 c. 19. 1957 c. 53.

(2) Section 67(9) above shall not have effect in relation to investigations of offences conducted under the Army Act 1955, the Air Force Act 1955 or the Naval Discipline Act 1957.

(3) The Secretary of State shall issue a code of practice, or a number of such codes, for persons other than police officers who are concerned with enquiries into offences under the Army Act 1955, the Air Force Act 1955 or the Naval Discipline Act 1957.

PART XI

(4) Without prejudice to the generality of subsection (3) above, a code issued under that subsection may contain provisions, in connection with enquiries into such offences, as to the following matters—

(a) the tape-recording of interviews;

(b) searches of persons and premises; and

(c) the seizure of things found on searches.

(5) If the Secretary of State lays before both Houses of Parliament a draft of a code of practice under this section, he may by order bring the code into operation.

(6) An order bringing a code of practice into operation may contain such transitional provisions or savings as appear to the Secretary of State to be necessary or expedient in connection with the code of practice thereby brought into operation.

(7) The Secretary of State may from time to time revise the whole or any part of a code of practice issued under this section and issue that revised code, and the foregoing provisions of this section shall apply (with appropriate modifications) to such a revised code as they apply to the first issue of a code.

(8) A failure on the part of any person to comply with any provision of a code of practice issued under this section shall not of itself render him liable to any criminal or civil proceedings except those to which this subsection applies.

(9) Subsection (8) above applies—

1955 c. 18.
1955 c. 19.

(a) to proceedings under any provision of the Army Act 1955 or the Air Force Act 1955 other than section 70; and

1957 c. 53.

(b) to proceedings under any provision of the Naval Discipline Act 1957 other than section 42.

(10) In all criminal and civil proceedings any such code shall be admissible in evidence and if any provision of such a code appears to the court or tribunal conducting the proceedings to be relevant to any question arising in the proceedings it shall be taken into account in determining that question.

(11) In subsection (10) above "criminal proceedings" includes—

(a) proceedings in the United Kingdom or elsewhere before a court-martial constituted under the Army Act 1955, the Air Force Act 1955 or the Naval Discipline Act 1957 or a disciplinary court constituted under section 50 of the said Act of 1957;

(b) proceedings before the Courts-Martial Appeal Court; and

(c) proceedings before a Standing Civilian Court.

(12) Parts VII and VIII of this Act have effect for the purposes of proceedings—

(a) before a court-martial constituted under the Army Act 1955 or the Air Force Act 1955;

(b) before the Courts-Martial Appeal Court; and

(c) before a Standing Civilian Court,

subject to any modifications which the Secretary of State may by order specify.

(13) An order under this section shall be made by statutory instrument and shall be subject to annulment in pursuance of a resolution of either House of Parliament.

1955 c. 18.
1955 c. 19.

114.—(1) " Arrested ", " arresting ", " arrest " and " to arrest " shall respectively be substituted for " detained ", " detaining ", " detention " and " to detain " wherever in the customs and excise Acts, as defined in section 1(1) of the Customs and Excise Management Act 1979, those words are used in relation to persons.

Application of Act to Customs and Excise.
1979 c. 2.

(2) The Treasury may by order direct—

(a) that any provision of this Act which relates to investigations of offences conducted by police officers or to persons detained by the police shall apply, subject to such modifications as the order may specify, to investigations conducted by officers of Customs and Excise of offences which relate to assigned matters, as defined in section 1 of the Customs and Excise Management Act 1979, or to persons detained by officers of Customs and Excise; and

(b) that, in relation to investigations of offences conducted by officers of Customs and Excise—

(i) this Act shall have effect as if the following section were inserted after section 14—

" Exception for Customs and Excise.

14A. Material in the possession of a person who acquired or created it in the course of any trade, business, profession or other occupation or for the purpose of any paid or unpaid office and which relates to an assigned matter, as defined in section 1 of the Customs and Excise Management Act 1979, is neither excluded material nor special procedure material for the purposes of any enactment such as is mentioned in section 9(2) above."; and

(ii) section 55 above shall have effect as if it related only to things such as are mentioned in subsection (1)(*a*) of that section.

(3) Nothing in any order under subsection (2) above shall be taken to limit any powers exercisable under section 164 of the Customs and Excise Management Act 1979.

(4) In this section " officers of Customs and Excise " means officers commissioned by the Commissioners of Customs and Excise under section 6(3) of the Customs and Excise Management Act 1979.

(5) An order under this section shall be made by statutory instrument and shall be subject to annulment in pursuance of a resolution of either House of Parliament.

Expenses.

115. Any expenses of a Minister of the Crown incurred in consequence of the provisions of this Act, including any increase attributable to those provisions in sums payable under any other Act, shall be defrayed out of money provided by Parliament.

Meaning of " serious arrestable offence ".

116.—(1) This section has effect for determining whether an offence is a serious arrestable offence for the purposes of this Act.

(2) The following arrestable offences are always serious—

(*a*) an offence (whether at common law or under any enactment) specified in Part I of Schedule 5 to this Act; and

(*b*) an offence under an enactment specified in Part II of that Schedule.

(3) Subject to subsections (4) and (5) below, any other arrestable offence is serious only if its commission—

(*a*) has led to any of the consequences specified in subsection (6) below; or

(*b*) is intended or is likely to lead to any of those consequences.

(4) An arrestable offence which consists of making a threat is serious if carrying out the threat would be likely to lead to any of the consequences specified in subsection (6) below.

(5) An offence under section 1, 9 or 10 of the Prevention of Terrorism (Temporary Provisions) Act 1984 is always a serious arrestable offence for the purposes of section 56 or 58 above,

and an attempt or conspiracy to commit any such offence is also always a serious arrestable offence for those purposes.

(6) The consequences mentioned in subsections (3) and (4) above are
- (a) serious harm to the security of the State or to public order;
- (b) serious interference with the administration of justice or with the investigation of offences or of a particular offence;
- (c) the death of any person;
- (d) serious injury to any person;
- (e) substantial financial gain to any person; and
- (f) serious financial loss to any person.

(7) Loss is serious for the purposes of this section if, having regard to all the circumstances, it is serious for the person who suffers it.

(8) In this section "injury" includes any disease and any impairment of a person's physical or mental condition.

117. Where any provision of this Act—
- (a) confers a power on a constable; and
- (b) does not provide that the power may only be exercised with the consent of some person, other than a police officer,

the officer may use reasonable force, if necessary, in the exercise of the power.

118.—(1) In this Act—
"arrestable offence" has the meaning assigned to it by section 24 above;

"designated police station" has the meaning assigned to it by section 35 above;

"document" has the same meaning as in Part I of the Civil Evidence Act 1968;

"intimate search" means a search which consists of the physical examination of a person's body orifices;

"item subject to legal privilege" has the meaning assigned to it by section 10 above;

"parent or guardian" means—
  (a) in the case of a child or young person in the care of a local authority, that authority; and
  (b) in the case of a child or young person in the care of a voluntary organisation in which parental rights and duties with respect to him are vested by

PART XI
1980 c. 5.

virtue of a resolution under section 64(1) of the Child Care Act 1980, that organisation;

"premises" has the meaning assigned to it by section 23 above;

"recordable offence" means any offence to which regulations under section 27 above apply;

"vessel" includes any ship, boat, raft or other apparatus constructed or adapted for floating on water.

(2) A person is in police detention for the purposes of this Act if—

(a) he has been taken to a police station after being arrested for an offence; or

(b) he is arrested at a police station after attending voluntarily at the station or accompanying a constable to it,

and is detained there or is detained elsewhere in the charge of a constable, except that a person who is at a court after being charged is not in police detention for those purposes.

Amendments and repeals.

119.—(1) The enactments mentioned in Schedule 6 to this Act shall have effect with the amendments there specified.

(2) The enactments mentioned in Schedule 7 to this Act (which include enactments already obsolete or unnecessary) are repealed to the extent specified in the third column of that Schedule.

(3) The repeals in Parts II and IV of Schedule 7 to this Act have effect only in relation to criminal proceedings.

Extent.

120.—(1) Subject to the following provisions of this section, this Act extends to England and Wales only.

(2) The following extend to Scotland only—
section 108(4) and (5);
section 110;
section 111;
section 112(1); and
section 119(2), so far as it relates to the provisions of the Pedlars Act 1871 repealed by Part VI of Schedule 7.

1871 c. 96.

(3) The following extend to Northern Ireland only—
section 6(4); and
section 112(2).

(4) The following extend to England and Wales and Scotland—
- section 6(1) and (2);
- section 7;
- section 83(2), so far as it relates to paragraph 8 of Schedule 4;
- section 108(1) and (6);
- section 109; and
- section 119(2), so far as it relates to section 19 of the Pedlars Act 1871.

1871 c. 96.

(5) The following extend to England and Wales, Scotland and Northern Ireland—
- section 6(3);
- section 83(2), so far as it relates to paragraph 7(1) of Schedule 4; and
- section 114(1).

(6) So far as they relate to proceedings before courts-martial and Standing Civilian Courts, the relevant provisions extend to any place at which such proceedings may be held.

(7) So far as they relate to proceedings before the Courts-Martial Appeal Court, the relevant provisions extend to any place at which such proceedings may be held.

(8) In this section " the relevant provisions " means—
- (a) subsection (11) of section 67 above;
- (b) subsection (12) of that section so far as it relates to subsection (11);
- (c) Parts VII and VIII of this Act, except paragraph 10 of Schedule 3;
- (d) subsections (2) and (8) to (12) of section 113 above; and
- (e) subsection (13) of that section, so far as it relates to an order under subsection (12).

(9) Except as provided by the foregoing provisions of this section, section 113 above extends to any place to which the Army Act 1955, the Air Force Act 1955 or the Naval Discipline Act 1957 extends.

1955 c. 18.
1955 c. 19.
1957 c. 53.

(9) Section 119(1), so far as it relates to any provision amended by Part II of Schedule 6, extends to any place to which that provision extends.

PART XI

(10) Section 119(2), so far as it relates—
  (a) to any provision contained in—
1955 c. 18.   the Army Act 1955;
1955 c. 19.   the Air Force Act 1955;
1981 c. 55.   the Armed Forces Act 1981; or
1983 c. 55.   the Value Added Tax Act 1983;
  (b) to any provision mentioned in Part VI of Schedule 7,
1871 c. 96.   other than section 18 of the Pedlars Act 1871,
extends to any place to which that provision extends.

(11) So far as any of the following—
section 115;
in section 118, the definition of "document";
this section;
section 121; and
section 122,
has effect in relation to any other provision of this Act, it extends to any place to which that provision extends.

Commencement.

121.—(1) This Act, except section 120 above, this section and section 122 below, shall come into operation on such day as the Secretary of State may by order made by statutory instrument appoint, and different days may be so appointed for different provisions and for different purposes.

(2) Different days may be appointed under this section for the coming into force of section 60 above in different areas.

(3) When an order under this section provides by virtue of subsection (2) above that section 60 above shall come into force in an area specified in the order, the duty imposed on the Secretary of State by that section shall be construed as a duty to make an order under it in relation to interviews in that area.

(4) An order under this section may make such transitional provision as appears to the Secretary of State to be necessary or expedient in connection with the provisions thereby brought into operation.

Short title.

122. This Act may be cited as the Police and Criminal Evidence Act 1984.

SCHEDULES

SCHEDULE 1

Special Procedure

Making of orders by circuit judge

1. If on an application made by a constable a circuit judge is satisfied that one or other of the sets of access conditions is fulfilled, he may make an order under paragraph 4 below.

2. The first set of access conditions is fulfilled if—
   (a) there are reasonable grounds for believing—
      (i) that a serious arrestable offence has been committed;
      (ii) that there is material which consists of special procedure material or includes special procedure material and does not also include excluded material on premises specified in the application;
      (iii) that the material is likely to be of substantial value (whether by itself or together with other material) to the investigation in connection with which the application is made; and
      (iv) that the material is likely to be relevant evidence;
   (b) other methods of obtaining the material—
      (i) have been tried without success; or
      (ii) have not been tried because it appeared that they were bound to fail; and
   (c) it is in the public interest, having regard—
      (i) to the benefit likely to accrue to the investigation if the material is obtained; and
      (ii) to the circumstances under which the person in possession of the material holds it,
   that the material should be produced or that access to it should be given.

3. The second set of access conditions is fulfilled if—
   (a) there are reasonable grounds for believing that there is material which consists of or includes excluded material or special procedure material on premises specified in the application;
   (b) but for section 9(2) above a search of the premises for that material could have been authorised by the issue of a warrant to a constable under an enactment other than this Schedule; and
   (c) the issue of such a warrant would have been appropriate.

4. An order under this paragraph is an order that the person who appears to the circuit judge to be in possession of the material to which the application relates shall—
   (a) produce it to a constable for him to take away; or
   (b) give a constable access to it,
not later than the end of the period of seven days from the date of the order or the end of such longer period as the order may specify.

SCH. 1

5. Where the material consists of information contained in a computer—
   (a) an order under paragraph 4(a) above shall have effect as an order to produce the material in a form in which it can be taken away and in which it is visible and legible; and
   (b) an order under paragraph 4(b) above shall have effect as an order to give a constable access to the material in a form in which it is visible and legible.

6. For the purposes of sections 21 and 22 above material produced in pursuance of an order under paragraph 4(a) above shall be treated as if it were material seized by a constable.

Notices of applications for orders

7. An application for an order under paragraph 4 above shall be made inter partes.

8. Notice of an application for such an order may be served on a person either by delivering it to him or by leaving it at his proper address or by sending it by post to him in a registered letter or by the recorded delivery service.

9. Such a notice may be served—
   (a) on a body corporate, by serving it on the body's secretary or clerk or other similar officer; and
   (b) on a partnership, by serving it on one of the partners.

1978 c. 30.

10. For the purposes of this Schedule, and of section 7 of the Interpretation Act 1978 in its application to this Schedule, the proper address of a person, in the case of secretary or clerk or other similar officer of a body corporate, shall be that of the registered or principal office of that body, in the case of a partner of a firm shall be that of the principal office of the firm, and in any other case shall be the last known address of the person to be served.

11. Where notice of an application for an order under paragraph 4 above has been served on a person, he shall not conceal, destroy, alter or dispose of the material to which the application relates except—
   (a) with the leave of a judge; or
   (b) with the written permission of a constable,
until—
   (i) the application is dismissed or abandoned; or
   (ii) he has complied with an order under paragraph 4 above made on the application.

Issue of warrants by circuit judge

12. If on an application made by a constable a circuit judge—
   (a) is satisfied—
      (i) that either set of access conditions is fulfilled; and
      (ii) that any of the further conditions set out in paragraph 14 below is also fulfilled; or

(b) is satisfied—

(i) that the second set of access conditions is fulfilled; and

(ii) that an order under paragraph 4 above relating to the material has not been complied with,

he may issue a warrant authorising a constable to enter and search the premises.

13. A constable may seize and retain anything for which a search has been authorised under paragraph 12 above.

14. The further conditions mentioned in paragraph 12(a)(ii) above are—

(a) that it is not practicable to communicate with any person entitled to grant entry to the premises to which the application relates;

(b) that it is practicable to communicate with a person entitled to grant entry to the premises but it is not practicable to communicate with any person entitled to grant access to the material;

(c) that the material contains information which—

(i) is subject to a restriction or obligation such as is mentioned in section 11(2)(b) above; and

(ii) is likely to be disclosed in breach of it if a warrant is not issued;

(d) that service of notice of an application for an order under paragraph 4 above may seriously prejudice the investigation.

15.—(1) If a person fails to comply with an order under paragraph 4 above, a circuit judge may deal with him as if he had committed a contempt of the Crown Court.

(2) Any enactment relating to contempt of the Crown Court shall have effect in relation to such a failure as if it were such a contempt.

Costs

16. The costs of any application under this Schedule and of anything done or to be done in pursuance of an order made under it shall be in the discretion of the judge.

SCHEDULE 2

PRESERVED POWERS OF ARREST

1892 c.43.	Section 17(2) of the Military Lands Act 1892.
1911 c.27.	Section 12(1) of the Protection of Animals Act 1911.
1920 c.55.	Section 2 of the Emergency Powers Act 1920.
1936 c.6.	Section 7(3) of the Public Order Act 1936.

SCH. 2

1952 c.52.	Section 49 of the Prison Act 1952.
1952 c.67.	Section 13 of the Visiting Forces Act 1952.
1955 c.18.	Sections 186 and 190B of the Army Act 1955.
1955 c.19.	Section 186 and 190B of the Air Force Act 1955.
1957 c.53.	Sections 104 and 105 of the Naval Discipline Act 1957.
1959 c.37.	Section 1(3) of the Street Offences Act 1959.
1969 c.54.	Sections 28(2) and 32 of the Children and Young Persons Act 1969.
1971 c.77.	Section 24(2) of the Immigration Act 1971 and paragraphs 17, 24 and 33 of Schedule 2 and paragraph 7 of Schedule 3 to that Act.
1972 c.20.	Sections 5(5), 7 and 100 of the Road Traffic Act 1972.
1976 c.63.	Section 7 of the Bail Act 1976.
1977 c.45.	Sections 6(6), 7(11), 8(4), 9(7) and 10(5) of the Criminal Law Act 1977.
1980 c.5.	Section 16 of the Child Care Act 1980.
1980 c.9.	Schedule 5 to the Reserve Forces Act 1980.
1981 c.22.	Sections 60(5) and 61(1) of the Animal Health Act 1981.
1983 c.20.	Sections 18, 35(10), 36(8), 38(7), 136(1) and 138 of the Mental Health Act 1983.
1984 c.8.	Sections 12 and 13 of the Prevention of Terrorism (Temporary Provisions) Act 1984.
1984 c.47.	Section 5(5) of the Repatriation of Prisoners Act 1984.

Section 70.

SCHEDULE 3

PROVISIONS SUPPLEMENTARY TO SECTIONS 68 AND 69

PART I

PROVISIONS SUPPLEMENTARY TO SECTION 68

1. Section 68(1) above applies whether the information contained in the document was supplied directly or indirectly but, if it was supplied indirectly, only if each person through whom it was supplied was acting under a duty; and applies also where the person compiling the record is himself the person by whom the information is supplied.

2. Where—
   (a) a document setting out the evidence which a person could be expected to give as a witness has been prepared for the purpose of any pending or contemplated proceedings; and
   (b) it falls within subsection (1) of section 68 above,

a statement contained in it shall not be given in evidence by virtue of that section without the leave of the court, and the court shall not give leave unless it is of the opinion that the statement ought to be admitted in the interests of justice, having regard—

   (i) to the circumstances in which leave is sought and in particular to the contents of the statement; and

(ii) to any likelihood that the accused will be prejudiced by its admission in the absence of the person who supplied the information on which it is based.

3. Where in any proceedings a statement based on information supplied by any person is given in evidence by virtue of section 68 above—

(a) any evidence which, if that person had been called as a witness, would have been admissible as relevant to his credibility as a witness shall be admissible for that purpose in those proceedings;

(b) evidence may, with the leave of the court, be given of any matter which, if that person had been called as a witness, could have been put to him in cross-examination as relevant to his credibility as a witness but of which evidence could not have been adduced by the cross-examining party; and

(c) evidence tending to prove that that person, whether before or after supplying the information, made a statement (whether oral or not) which is inconsistent with it shall be admissible for the purpose of showing that he has contradicted himself.

4. A statement which is admissible by virtue of section 68 above shall not be capable of corroborating evidence given by the person who supplied the information on which the statement is based.

5. In deciding for the purposes of section 68(2)(a)(i) above whether a person is unfit to attend as a witness the court may act on a certificate purporting to be signed by a registered medical practitioner.

6. Any reference in section 68 above or this Part of this Schedule to a person acting under a duty includes a reference to a person acting in the course of any trade, business, profession or other occupation in which he is engaged or employed or for the purposes of any paid or unpaid office held by him.

7. In estimating the weight, if any, to be attached to a statement admissible in evidence by virtue of section 68 above regard shall be had to all the circumstances from which any inference can reasonably be drawn as to the accuracy or otherwise of the statement and, in particular—

(a) to the question whether or not the person who supplied the information from which the record containing the statement was compiled did so contemporaneously with the occurrence or existence of the facts dealt with in that information; and

(b) to the question whether or not that person, or any other person concerned with compiling or keeping the record containing the statement, had any incentive to conceal or misrepresent the facts.

PART II

PROVISIONS SUPPLEMENTARY TO SECTION 69

8. In any proceedings where it is desired to give a statement in evidence in accordance with section 69 above, a certificate—

   (a) identifying the document containing the statement and describing the manner in which it was produced;

   (b) giving such particulars of any device involved in the production of that document as may be appropriate for the purpose of showing that the document was produced by a computer;

   (c) dealing with any of the matters mentioned in subsection (1) of section 69 above; and

   (d) purporting to be signed by a person occupying a responsible position in relation to the operation of the computer,

shall be evidence of anything stated in it; and for the purposes of this paragraph it shall be sufficient for a matter to be stated to the best of the knowledge and belief of the person stating it.

9. Notwithstanding paragraph 8 above, a court may require oral evidence to be given of anything of which evidence could be given by a certificate under that paragraph.

10. Any person who in a certificate tendered under paragraph 8 above in a magistrates' court, the Crown Court or the Court of Appeal makes a statement which he knows to be false or does not believe to be true shall be guilty of an offence and liable—

    (a) on conviction on indictment to imprisonment for a term not exceeding two years or to a fine or to both;

    (b) on summary conviction to imprisonment for a term not exceeding six months or to a fine not exceeding the statutory maximum (as defined in section 74 of the Criminal Justice Act 1982) or to both.

11. In estimating the weight, if any, to be attached to a statement regard shall be had to all the circumstances from which any inference can reasonably be drawn as to the accuracy or otherwise of the statement and, in particular—

    (a) to the question whether or not the information which the information contained in the statement reproduces or is derived from was supplied to the relevant computer, or recorded for the purpose of being supplied to it, contemporaneously with the occurrence or existence of the facts dealt with in that information; and

    (b) to the question whether or not any person concerned with the supply of information to that computer, or with the operation of that computer or any equipment by means of which the document containing the statement was produced by it, had any incentive to conceal or misrepresent the facts.

12. For the purposes of paragraph 11 above information shall be taken to be supplied to a computer whether it is supplied directly

or (with or without human intervention) by means of any appropriate equipment.

PART III

PROVISIONS SUPPLEMENTARY TO SECTIONS 68 AND 69

13. Where in any proceedings a statement contained in a document is admissible in evidence by virtue of section 68 above or in accordance with section 69 above it may be proved—

(a) by the production of that document ; or

(b) (whether or not that document is still in existence) by the production of a copy of that document, or of the material part of it,

authenticated in such manner as the court may approve.

14. For the purpose of deciding whether or not a statement is so admissible the court may draw any reasonable inference—

(a) from the circumstances in which the statement was made or otherwise came into being ; or

(b) from any other circumstances, including the form and contents of the document in which the statement is contained.

15. Provision may be made by rules of court for supplementing the provisions of section 68 or 69 above or this Schedule.

SCHEDULE 4

THE POLICE COMPLAINTS AUTHORITY

PART I

GENERAL

Constitution of Authority

1.—(1) The Police Complaints Authority shall consist of a chairman and not less than 8 other members.

(2) The chairman shall be appointed by Her Majesty.

(3) The other members shall be appointed by the Secretary of State.

(4) The members of the Authority shall not include any person who is or has been a constable in any part of the United Kingdom.

(5) Persons may be appointed as whole-time or part-time members of the Authority.

(6) The Secretary of State shall appoint 2 of the members of the Authority to be deputy chairmen of the Authority.

Incorporation and status of Authority

2.—(1) The Authority shall be a body corporate.

(2) It is hereby declared that the Authority are not to be regarded as the servant or agent of the Crown or as enjoying any

Sch. 4

status, privilege or immunity of the Crown; and the Authority's property shall not be regarded as property of or property held on behalf of the Crown.

Members

3.—(1) Subject to the following provisions of this Schedule, a person shall hold an office to which he is appointed under paragraph 1(2), (3) or (6) above in accordance with the terms of his appointment.

(2) A person shall not be appointed to such an office for more than 3 years at a time.

(3) A person may at any time resign such an office.

(4) The Secretary of State may at any time remove a person from such an office if satisfied that—

(a) he has without reasonable excuse failed to carry out his duties for a continuous period of 3 months beginning not earlier than 6 months before that time; or

(b) he has been convicted of a criminal offence; or

(c) he has become bankrupt or made an arrangement with his creditors; or

(d) he is incapacitated by physical or mental illness; or

(e) he is otherwise unable or unfit to perform his duties.

4. The Secretary of State may pay, or make such payments towards the provision of, such remuneration, pensions, allowances or gratuities to or in respect of persons appointed to office under paragraph 1(2), (3) or (6) above or any of them as, with the consent of the Treasury, he may determine.

5. Where a person ceases to hold such an office otherwise than on the expiry of his term of office, and it appears to the Secretary of State that there are special circumstances which make it right for that person to receive compensation, the Secretary of State may, with the consent of the Treasury, direct the Authority to make to the person a payment of such amount as, with the consent of the Treasury, the Secretary of State may determine.

Staff

6. The Authority may, after consultation with the Secretary of State, appoint such officers and servants as the Authority think fit, subject to the approval of the Treasury as to numbers and as to remuneration and other terms and conditions of service.

7.—(1) Employment by the Authority shall be included among the kinds of employment to which a superannuation scheme under section 1 of the Superannuation Act 1972 can apply, and accordingly in Schedule 1 to that Act, at the end of the list of "Other Bodies" there shall be inserted—

"Police Complaints Authority".

(2) Where a person who is employed by the Authority and is by reference to that employment a participant in a scheme under

1972 c. 11.

section 1 of the said Act of 1972 is appointed to an office under paragraph 1(2), (3) or (6) above the Treasury may determine that his service in that office shall be treated for the purposes of the scheme as service as an employee of the Authority; and his rights under the scheme shall not be affected by paragraph 4 above.

SCH. 4

8. The Employers' Liability (Compulsory Insurance) Act 1969 shall not require insurance to be effected by the Authority.

1969 c. 57.

Power of Authority to set up regional offices

9.—(1) If it appears to the Authority that it is necessary to do so in order to discharge their duties efficiently, the Authority may, with the consent of the Secretary of State and the Treasury, set up a regional office in any place in England and Wales.

(2) The Authority may delegate any of their functions to a regional office.

Proceedings

10.—(1) Subject to the provisions of this Act, the arrangements for the proceedings of the Authority (including the quorum for meetings) shall be such as the Authority may determine.

(2) The arrangements may, with the approval of the Secretary of State, provide for the discharge, under the general direction of the Authority, of any of the Authority's functions by a committee or by one or more of the members, officers or servants of the Authority.

11. The validity of any proceedings of the Authority shall not be affected—
   (a) by any defect in the appointment—
      (i) of the chairman;
      (ii) of a deputy chairman; or
      (iii) of any other member; or
   (b) by any vacancy—
      (i) in the office of chairman;
      (ii) among the other members; or
      (iii) in the office of deputy chairman.

Finance

12. The Secretary of State shall pay to the Authority expenses incurred or to be incurred by the Authority under paragraphs 5 and 6 above and, with the consent of the Treasury, shall pay to the Authority such sums as the Secretary of State thinks fit for enabling the Authority to meet other expenses.

13.—(1) It shall be the duty of the Authority—
   (a) to keep proper accounts and proper records in relation to the accounts;
   (b) to prepare in respect of each financial year of the Authority a statement of accounts in such form as the Secretary of State may direct with the approval of the Treasury; and

Sch. 4

(c) to send copies of the statement to the Secretary of State and the Comptroller and Auditor General before the end of the month of August next following the financial year to which the statement relates.

(2) The Comptroller and Auditor General shall examine, certify and report on each statement received by him in pursuance of this paragraph and shall lay copies of each statement and of his report before Parliament.

(3) The financial year of the Authority shall be the 12 months ending on 31st March.

Part II

Transitional

Information received by Police Complaints Board

14.—(1) No information received by the Police Complaints Board in connection with any complaint shall be disclosed by any person who has been a member, officer or servant of the Board except—

(a) to the Secretary of State or to a member, officer or servant of the Authority or, so far as may be necessary for the proper discharge of the functions of the Authority, to other persons; or

(b) for the purposes of any criminal, civil or disciplinary proceedings.

(2) Any person who discloses information in contravention of this paragraph shall be guilty of an offence and liable on summary conviction to a fine of an amount not exceeding level 5 on the standard scale, as defined in section 75 of the Criminal Justice Act 1982.

1982 c. 48.

Property, rights and liabilities

15.—(1) On the day on which section 83 above comes into operation all property, rights and liabilities which immediately before that day were property, rights and liabilities of the Police Complaints Board shall vest in the Authority by virtue of this paragraph and without further assurance.

1895 c. 16.

(2) Section 12 of the Finance Act 1895 (which requires Acts to be stamped as conveyances on sale in certain cases) shall not apply to any transfer of property effected by this paragraph.

Proceedings

16. Proceedings in any court to which the Police Complaints Board is a party and which are pending immediately before the date on which section 83 above comes into operation may be continued on and after that day by the Authority.

Payments to former members of Police Complaints Board   SCH. 4

17. Where a person—
   (a) ceases to be a member of the Police Complaints Board by reason of its abolition; and
   (b) does not become a member of the Authority,

the Secretary of State may, with the consent of the Treasury, make to the person a payment of such amount as, with the consent of the Treasury, the Secretary of State may determine.

General

18. Paragraphs 14 to 17 above are without prejudice to the generality of section 121(4) above.

SCHEDULE 5

Section 116.

SERIOUS ARRESTABLE OFFENCES

PART I

OFFENCES MENTIONED IN SECTION 116(2)(a)

1. Treason.
2. Murder.
3. Manslaughter.
4. Rape.
5. Kidnapping.
6. Incest with a girl under the age of 13.
7. Buggery with—
   (a) a boy under the age of 16; or
   (b) a person who has not consented.
8. Indecent assault which constitutes an act of gross indecency.

PART II

OFFENCES MENTIONED IN SECTION 116(2)(b)

Explosive Substances Act 1883 (c. 3)

1. Section 2 (causing explosion likely to endanger life or property).

Sexual Offences Act 1956 (c. 69)

2. Section 5 (intercourse with a girl under the age of 13).

Firearms Act 1968 (c. 27)

3. Section 16 (possession of firearms with intent to injure).
4. Section 17(1) (use of firearms and imitation firearms to resist arrest).
5. Section 18 (carrying firearms with criminal intent).

Police and Criminal Evidence Act 1984

SCH. 5

Road Traffic Act 1972 (c. 20)

6. Section 1 (causing death by reckless driving).

Taking of Hostages Act 1982 (c. 28)

7. Section 1 (hostage-taking).

Aviation Security Act 1982 (c. 36)

8. Section 1 (hi-jacking).

Section 119.

SCHEDULE 6

Minor and Consequential Amendments

Part I

England and Wales

Game Act 1831 (c. 32)

1. The following section shall be inserted after section 31 of the Game Act 1831—

"Powers of constables in relation to trespassers.

31A. The powers conferred by section 31 above to require a person found on land as mentioned in that section to quit the land and to tell his christian name, surname, and place of abode shall also be exercisable by a police constable.".

Metropolitan Police Act 1839 (c. 47)

2. In section 39 of the Metropolitan Police Act 1839 (fairs within the metropolitan police district) after the word "amusement" there shall be inserted the words "shall be guilty of an offence".

Railway Regulation Act 1840 (c. 97)

3. In section 16 of the Railway Regulation Act 1840 (persons obstructing officers of railway company or trespassing upon railway) for the words from "and" in the third place where it occurs to "justice," in the third place where it occurs there shall be substituted the words ", upon conviction by a magistrates' court, at the discretion of the court,".

London Hackney Carriages Act 1843 (c. 86)

4. In section 27 of the London Hackney Carriages Act 1843 (no person to act as driver of carriage without consent of proprietor) for the words after "constable" there shall be substituted the words "if necessary, to take charge of the carriage and every horse in charge of any person unlawfully acting as a driver and to deposit the same in some place of safe custody until the same can be applied for by the proprietor.".

Town Gardens Protection Act 1863 (c. 13)

5. In section 5 of the Town Gardens Protection Act 1863 (penalty for injuring garden) for the words from the beginning to "district"

there shall be substituted the words "Any person who throws any rubbish into any such garden, or trespasses therein, or gets over the railings or fence, or steals or damages the flowers or plants, or commits any nuisance therein, shall be guilty of an offence and".

Parks Regulation Act 1872 (c. 15)

6. The following section shall be substituted for section 5 of the Parks Regulation Act 1872 (apprehension of offender whose name or residence is not known)—

"5. Any person who—

(a) within the view of a park constable acts in contravention of any of the said regulations in the park where the park constable has jurisdiction; and

(b) when required by any park constable or by any police constable to give his name and address gives a false name or false address,

shall be liable on summary conviction to a penalty of an amount not exceeding level 1 on the standard scale, as defined in section 75 of the Criminal Justice Act 1982.".

Dogs (Protection of Livestock) Act 1953 (c. 28)

7. In the Dogs (Protection of Livestock) Act 1953 the following section shall be inserted after section 2—

"Power of justice of the peace to authorise entry and search.

2A. If on an application made by a constable a justice of the peace is satisfied that there are reasonable grounds for believing—

(a) that an offence under this Act has been committed; and

(b) that the dog in respect of which the offence has been commited is on premises specified in the application,

he may issue a warrant authorising a constable to enter and search the premises in order to identify the dog.".

Army Act 1955 (c. 18)
Air Force Act 1955 (c. 19)

8. The following subsection shall be substituted for section 195(3) of the Army Act 1955 and section 195(3) of the Air Force Act 1955—

"(3) A constable may seize any property which he has reasonable grounds for suspecting of having been the subject of an offence against this section.".

Sexual Offences Act 1956 (c. 69)

9. At the end of section 41 of the Sexual Offences Act 1956 (power to arrest in cases of soliciting by men) there shall be added the words "but a constable may only do so in accordance with section 25 of the Police and Criminal Evidence Act 1984.".

Sch. 6

Game Laws (Amendment) Act 1960 (c. 36)

10. In subsection (1) of section 2 of the Game Laws (Amendment) Act 1960 (power of police to enter on land) for the words " purpose of exercising any power conferred on him by the foregoing section " there shall be substituted the words " purpose—

(a) of exercising in relation to him the powers under section 31 of the Game Act 1831 which section 31A of that Act confers on police constables ; or

(b) of arresting him in accordance with section 25 of the Police and Criminal Evidence Act 1984.".

11. In subsection (1) of section 4 of that Act (enforcement powers) for the words from " under ", in the first place where it occurs, to " thirty-one " there shall be substituted the words ", in accordance with section 25 of the Police and Criminal Evidence Act 1984, for an offence under section one or section nine of the Night Poaching Act 1828, or under section thirty ".

Betting, Gaming and Lotteries Act 1963 (c. 2)

12. The following subsection shall be substituted for subsection (2) of section 8 of the Betting, Gaming and Lotteries Act 1963 (prohibition of betting in streets and public places)—

" (2) Where a person is found committing an offence under this section, any constable may seize and detain any article liable to be forfeited under this section.".

Deer Act 1963 (c. 36)

13. In subsection (2) of section 5 of the Deer Act 1963 (enforcement powers) after the word " subsection " there shall be inserted the words " or arresting a person, in accordance with section 25 of the Police and Criminal Evidence Act 1984, for an offence under this Act ".

Police Act 1964 (c. 48)

14. In section 7(1) of the Police Act 1964 (other members of police forces) after the words " chief constable " there shall be inserted the words ", deputy chief constable ".

15. In section 29(2) of that Act (removal of chief constables) for the words " the deputy or an assistant chief constable " there shall be substituted the words " a deputy or assistant chief constable ".

16. In section 43(5) of that Act (central service) after the word " constabulary " there shall be inserted the words " or with the Police Complaints Authority ".

Criminal Law Act 1967 (c. 58)

17. The following subsection shall be inserted after section 4(1) of the Criminal Law Act 1967—

" (1A) In this section and section 5 below " arrestable offence " has the meaning assigned to it by section 24 of the Police and Criminal Evidence Act 1984.".

Theatres Act 1968 (c. 54)

18. In section 15(1) of the Theatres Act 1968 (powers of entry and inspection) for the words "fourteen days" there shall be substituted the words "one month".

Children and Young Persons Act 1969 (c. 54)

19. In the Children and Young Persons Act 1969—

    (a) in section 28(4), for the words "a police officer not below the rank of inspector or by the police officer in charge of" there shall be substituted the words "the custody officer at"; and

    (b) the following section shall be substituted for section 29—

"Recognisance on release of arrested child or young person.

29. A child or young person arrested in pursuance of a warrant shall not be released unless he or his parent or guardian (with or without sureties) enters into a recognisance for such amount as the custody officer at the police station where he is detained considers will secure his attendance at the hearing of the charge; and the recognisance entered into in pursuance of this section may, if the custody officer thinks fit, be conditioned for the attendance of the parent or guardian at the hearing in addition to the child or young person.".

Immigration Act 1971 (c. 77)

20. In section 25(3) of the Immigration Act 1971 for the words "A constable or" there shall be substituted the word "An".

Criminal Justice Act 1972 (c. 71)

21. In subsection (1) of section 34 of the Criminal Justice Act 1972 (powers of constable to take drunken offender to treatment centre) for the words from the beginning to "section the" there shall be substituted the words "On arresting an offender for an offence under—

    (a) section 12 of the Licensing Act 1872; or   1872 c. 94.
    (b) section 91(1) of the Criminal Justice Act 1967,   1967 c. 80.
a".

Child Care Act 1980 (c. 5)

22. In subsection (1)(b) of section 73 of the Child Care Act 1980 (provisions as to places of safety etc.) for the words "section 29(3) of the Children and Young Persons Act 1969" there shall be substituted the words "section 38(7) of the Police and Criminal Evidence Act 1984".

Deer Act 1980 (c. 49)

23. In subsection (2) of section 4 of the Deer Act 1980 (enforcement powers) after the word "above" there shall be inserted the words "or arresting a person, in accordance with section 25 of the Police and Criminal Evidence Act 1984, for an offence under this Act".

SCH. 6

Animal Health Act 1981 (*c.* 22)

24. In subsection (5) of section 60 of the Animal Health Act 1981 (enforcement powers) for the words "a constable or other officer" there shall be substituted the words "an officer other than a constable".

Wildlife and Countryside Act 1981 (*c.* 69)

25. In subsection (2) of section 19 of the Wildlife and Countryside Act 1981 (enforcement powers) after the words "subsection (1)" there shall be inserted the words "or arresting a person, in accordance with section 25 of the Police and Criminal Evidence Act 1984, for such an offence".

Mental Health Act 1983 (*c.* 20)

26. In section 135(4) of the Mental Health Act 1983 for the words "the constable to whom it is addressed", in both places where they occur, there shall be substituted the words "a constable".

Prevention of Terrorism (Temporary Provisions) Act 1984 (*c.* 8)

27. In paragraph 4 of Schedule 3 to the Prevention of Terrorism (Temporary Provisions) Act 1984 (search warrants)—

(*a*) in sub-paragraph (4)—

(i) for the word "If" there shall be substituted the words "Subject to sub-paragraph (4A) below, if"; and

(ii) at the end there shall be added the words "or which could have been so given but for section 9(2) of the Police and Criminal Evidence Act 1984"; and

(*b*) the following sub-paragraph shall be inserted after sub-paragraph (4)—

"(4A) An order given under sub-paragraph (4) above may not authorise a search for items subject to legal privilege within the meaning of section 10 of the Police and Criminal Evidence Act 1984.".

PART II

OTHER AMENDMENTS

Army Act 1955 (*c.* 18)

28.—(1) The Army Act 1955 shall be amended as follows.

(2) In section 99—

(*a*) in subsection (1), after the word "below" there shall be inserted the words "and to service modifications"; and

(*b*) the following subsections shall be inserted after that subsection—

"(1A) In this section "service modifications" means such modifications as the Secretary of State may by regulations made by statutory instrument prescribe, being

SCH. 6

modifications which appear to him to be necessary or proper for the purposes of proceedings before a court-martial; and it is hereby declared that in this section—

"rules" includes rules contained in or made by virtue of an enactment; and

"enactment" includes an enactment contained in an Act passed after this Act.

(1B) Regulations under subsection (1A) above may not modify section 99A below.

(1C) Regulations under subsection (1A) above shall be subject to annulment in pursuance of a resolution of either House of Parliament.".

(3) In section 99A(1) for the word "Section" there shall be substituted the words "Without prejudice to section 99 above, section".

(4) The following section shall be inserted after section 200—

False statements in computer record certificates.
200A.—(1) Any person who in a certificate tendered under paragraph 8 of Schedule 3 to the Police and Criminal Evidence Act 1984 (computer records) in evidence before a court-martial makes a statement which he knows to be false or does not believe to be true shall be guilty of an offence and liable—

(a) on conviction on indictment to imprisonment for a term not exceeding two years or to a fine or to both;

(b) on summary conviction to imprisonment for a term not exceeding six months or to a fine not exceeding the statutory maximum or to both.

(2) In this section "statutory maximum" has the meaning given by section 74 of the Criminal Justice Act 1982.". 1982 c. 48.

Air Force Act 1955 (c. 19)

29.—(1) The Air Force Act 1955 shall be amended as follows.

(2) In section 99—

(a) in subsection (1), after the word "below" there shall be inserted the words "and to service modifications"; and

(b) the following subsections shall be inserted after that subsection—

"(1A) In this section "service modifications" means such modifications as the Secretary of State may by regulations made by statutory instrument prescribe, being modifications which appear to him to be necessary or proper for the purposes of proceedings before a court-martial; and it is hereby declared that in this section—

"rules" includes rules contained in or made by virtue of an enactment; and

SCH. 6

"enactment" includes an enactment contained in an Act passed after this Act.

(1B) Regulations under subsection (1A) above may not modify section 99A below.

(1C) Regulations under subsection (1A) above shall be subject to annulment in pursuance of a resolution of either House of Parliament.".

(3) In section 99A(1) for the word "Section" there shall be substituted the words "Without prejudice to section 99 above, section".

(4) The following section shall be inserted after section 200—

"False statements in computer record certificates.

200A.—(1) Any person who in a certificate tendered under paragraph 8 of Schedule 3 to the Police and Criminal Evidence Act 1984 (computer records) in evidence before a court-martial makes a statement which he knows to be false or does not believe to be true shall be guilty of an offence and liable—

(a) on conviction on indictment to imprisonment for a term not exceeding two years or to a fine or to both;

(b) on summary conviction to imprisonment for a term not exceeding six months or to a fine not exceeding the statutory maximum or to both.

1982 c. 48.

(2) In this section "statutory maximum" has the meaning given by section 74 of the Criminal Justice Act 1982.".

Police (Scotland) Act 1967 (c. 77)

30. In section 6(2) of the Police (Scotland) Act 1967 (constables below rank of assistant chief constable) for the words "an assistant chief constable or a constable holding the office of deputy chief constable" there shall be substituted the words "a deputy chief constable or an assistant chief constable".

31. In section 7(1) of that Act (ranks) after the words "chief constable," there shall be inserted the words "deputy chief constable,".

32. In section 26(7) of that Act (disciplinary authority) immediately before the words "deputy chief constable" there shall be inserted the word "any".

33. In section 31(2) of that Act (compulsory retirement of chief constable etc.) for the words "the deputy or an assistant chief constable" there shall be substituted the words "a deputy or assistant chief constable".

SCH. 6

Courts-Martial (Appeals) Act 1968 (c. 20)

34.—(1) The following section shall be inserted after section 37 of the Courts-Martial (Appeals) Act 1968—

"False statements in computer record certificates.

37A.—(1) Any person who in a certificate tendered under paragraph 8 of Schedule 3 to the Police and Criminal Evidence Act 1984 (computer records) in evidence before the Appeal Court makes a statement which he knows to be false or does not believe to be true shall be guilty of an offence and liable—

(a) on conviction on indictment to imprisonment for a term not exceeding two years or to a fine or to both;

(b) on summary conviction to imprisonment for a term not exceeding six months or to a fine not exceeding the statutory maximum or to both.

(2) Proceedings for an offence under this section committed outside the United Kingdom may be taken, and the offence may for all incidental purposes be treated as having been committed, in any place in the United Kingdom.

(3) In this section "statutory maximum" has the meaning given by section 74 of the Criminal Justice Act 1982.". 1982 c. 48.

House of Commons Disqualification Act 1975 (c. 24)

Northern Ireland Assembly Disqualification Act 1975 (c. 25)

35. In Part II of Schedule 1 to the House of Commons Disqualification Act 1975 and Part II of Schedule 1 to the Northern Ireland Assembly Disqualification Act 1975 (bodies of which all members are disqualified under those Acts) there shall be inserted at the appropriate place in alphabetical order—

"The Police Complaints Authority".

Armed Forces Act 1976 (c. 52)

36. The following paragraph shall be inserted after paragraph 17 of Schedule 3 to the Armed Forces Act 1976 (Standing Civilian Courts)—

"17A. Section 200A of that Act (false statements in computer record certificates) shall have effect as if the reference to a court-martial in subsection (1) included a reference to a Standing Civilian Court.".

Customs and Excise Management Act 1979 (c. 2)

37. The following subsection shall be substituted for section 138(4) of the Customs and Excise Management Act 1979—

"(4) Where any person has been arrested by a person who is not an officer—

(a) by virtue of this section; or

(b) by virtue of section 24 of the Police and Criminal Evidence Act 1984 in its application to offences under the customs and excise Acts,

Sch. 6

the person arresting him shall give notice of the arrest to an officer at the nearest convenient office of customs and excise.".

38. In section 161 of that Act—

(a) in subsection (3), for the words from "that officer" to the end of the subsection there shall be substituted the words "any officer and any person accompanying an officer to enter and search the building or place named in the warrant within one month from that day"; and

(b) in subsection (4), for the words "person named in a warrant under subsection (3) above" there shall be substituted the words "other person so authorised".

Betting and Gaming Duties Act 1981 (c. 63)

39. In the following provisions of the Betting and Gaming Duties Act 1981, namely—

(a) section 15(2);

(b) paragraph 16(1) of Schedule 1;

(c) paragraph 17(1) of Schedule 3; and

(d) paragraph 17(1) of Schedule 4,

for the words "fourteen days" there shall be substituted the words "one month".

Car Tax Act 1983 (c. 53)

40. In paragraph 7(3) of Schedule 1 to the Car Tax Act 1983 for the words "fourteen days" there shall be substituted the words "one month".

Value Added Tax Act 1983 (c. 55)

41. In Schedule 7 to the Value-Added Tax Act 1983—

(a) the following sub-paragraph shall be substituted for paragraph 7(5)—

"(5) A statement contained in a document produced by a computer shall not by virtue of sub-paragraph (3) of this paragraph be admissible in evidence—

(a) in civil proceedings in England and Wales, except in accordance with sections 5 and 6 of the Civil Evidence Act 1968;

1968 c. 64.

(b) in criminal proceedings in England and Wales except in accordance with sections 68 to 70 of the Police and Criminal Evidence Act 1984;

(c) in civil proceedings in Scotland, except in accordance with sections 13 and 14 of the Law Reform (Miscellaneous Provisions) (Scotland) Act 1968;

1968 c. 70.

(d) in criminal proceedings in Scotland, except in accordance with the said sections 13 and 14, which shall, for the purposes of this paragraph, apply with the necessary modifications to such proceedings;

(e) in civil proceedings in Northern Ireland, except in accordance with sections 2 and 3 of the

Civil Evidence Act (Northern Ireland) 1971; and

(f) in criminal proceedings in Northern Ireland, except in accordance with the said sections 2 and 3, which shall, for the purposes of this paragraph, apply with the necessary modifications to such proceedings.";

(b) in paragraph 7(6), for the words from " under the corresponding " to the end of the sub-paragraph there shall be substituted the words " section 13(4) of the Law Reform (Miscellaneous Provisions) (Scotland) Act 1968 or section 2(4) of the Civil Evidence Act (Northern Ireland) 1971 "; and

(c) in paragraph 10(3), for the words " 14 days " there shall be substituted the words " one month ".

SCH. 6
1971 c. 36 (N.I.).

1968 c. 70.

SCHEDULE 7

Section 119.

REPEALS

PART I

ENACTMENTS REPEALED IN CONSEQUENCE OF PARTS I TO V

Chapter	Short title	Extent of repeal
5 Geo. 4. c. 83.	Vagrancy Act 1824.	Section 8. Section 13.
1 & 2 Will. 4. c. 32.	Game Act 1831.	In section 31, the words " or for any police constable ".
2 & 3 Vict. c. 47.	Metropolitan Police Act 1839.	Section 34. In section 38, the words from " it " to " and " in the sixth place where it occurs. In section 39, the words " to take into custody ". In section 47, the words " take into custody " and the words ", and every person so found ". In section 54, the words from " And " to the end of the section. In section 62, the words from " may " in the first place where it occurs to " and " in the second place where it occurs. Sections 63 to 67.
3 & 4 Vict. c. 50.	Canals (Offences) Act 1840.	The whole Act.
5 & 6 Vict. c. 55.	Railway Regulation Act 1842.	In section 17, the words " or for any special constable duly appointed, ".
8 & 9 Vict. c. 20.	Railways Clauses Consolidation Act 1845.	In section 104, the words " and all constables, gaolers, and police officers, ".

SCH. 7

Chapter	Short title	Extent of repeal
10 & 11 Vict. c. 89.	Town Police Clauses Act 1847.	In section 15, the words " may be taken into custody, without a warrant, by any constable, or " and the words from " Provided " to the end of the section. In section 28, the words from " and " in the first place where it occurs to " offence " in the second place where it occurs.
14 & 15 Vict. c. 19.	Prevention of Offences Act 1851.	Section 11.
23 & 24 Vict. c. 32.	Ecclesiastical Courts Jurisdiction Act 1860.	In section 3, the words " constable or "
24 & 25 Vict. c. 100.	Offences against the Person Act 1861.	In section 65, the words " in the daytime ".
34 & 35 Vict. c. 96.	Pedlars Act 1871.	Sections 18 and 19.
35 & 36 Vict. c. 93.	Pawnbrokers Act 1872.	In section 36, the words ", within the hours of business,".
38 & 39 Vict. c. 17.	Explosives Act 1875.	In section 78, the words " a constable, or ".
52 & 53 Vict. c. 18.	Indecent Advertisements Act 1889.	Section 6.
52 & 53 Vict. c. 57.	Regulation of Railways Act 1889.	In section 5(2), the words " or any constable ".
8 Edw. 7. c. 66.	Public Meeting Act 1908.	In section 1, in subsection (3) the words from " and " in the sixth place where it occurs to the end of the subsection.
1 & 2 Geo. 5. c. 28.	Official Secrets Act 1911.	In section 9(1), the words " named therein ".
15 & 16 Geo. 5. c. 71.	Public Health Act 1925.	Section 74(2) and (3).
23 & 24 Geo. 5. c. 12.	Children and Young Persons Act 1933.	Section 10(2). Section 13(1) and (2). In section 40, in subsection (1) the words " named therein " and in subsection (4) the words " addressed to and ".
11 & 12 Geo. 6. c. 58.	Criminal Justice Act 1948.	Section 68.
1 & 2 Eliz. 2. c. 14.	Prevention of Crime Act 1953.	Section 1(3).
3 & 4 Eliz. 2. c. 28.	Children and Young Persons (Harmful Publications) Act 1955.	In section 3(1), the words " named therein ".
4 & 5 Eliz. 2. c. 69.	Sexual Offences Act 1956.	Section 40. In section 43(1), the word " named ".
5 & 6 Eliz. 2. c. 53.	Naval Discipline Act 1957.	In section 106(1), the words from " may " in the first place where it occurs to " and ".
7 & 8 Eliz. 2. c. 66.	Obscene Publications Act 1959.	In section 3(1), the words ", within fourteen days from the date of the warrant,".

SCH. 7

Chapter	Short title	Extent of repeal
8 & 9 Eliz. 2. c. 36.	Game Laws (Amendment) Act 1960.	Section 1.
1963 c. 2.	Betting, Gaming and Lotteries Act 1963.	In section 51(1), the words " at any time within fourteen days from the time of the issue of the warrant " and the words " arrest and ".
1963 c. 36.	Deer Act 1963.	Section 5(1)(c).
1964 c. 26.	Licensing Act 1964.	Section 187(5).
1967 c. 58.	Criminal Law Act 1967.	Section 2.
1968 c. 27.	Firearms Act 1968.	In section 46(1), the words " named therein ". Section 50.
1968 c. 52.	Caravan Sites Act 1968.	Section 11(5).
1968 c. 60.	Theft Act 1968.	Section 12(3). Section 26(2).
1968 c. 65.	Gaming Act 1968.	Section 5(2). In section 43, in subsection (4), the words " at any time within fourteen days from the time of the issue of the warrant ", and in subsection (5)(b), the words " arrest and ".
1970 c. 30.	Conservation of Seals Act 1970.	Section 4(1)(a).
1971 c. 38.	Misuse of Drugs Act 1971.	Section 24.
1971 c. 77.	Immigration Act 1971.	In Schedule 2, in paragraph 17(2), the words " acting for the police area in which the premises are situated," and the words " at any time or times within one month from the date of the warrant ".
1972 c. 20.	Road Traffic Act 1972.	Section 19(3). Section 164(2).
1972 c. 27.	Road Traffic (Foreign Vehicles) Act 1972.	Section 3(2).
1972 c. 71.	Criminal Justice Act 1972.	Section 34(3).
1973 c. 57.	Badgers Act 1973.	Section 10(1)(b).
1974 c. 6.	Biological Weapons Act 1974.	In section 4(1), the words " named therein ".
1976 c. 32.	Lotteries and Amusements Act 1976.	In section 19, the words " at any time within 14 days from the time of the issue of the warrant ".
1976 c. 58.	International Carriage of Perishable Foodstuffs Act 1976.	Section 11(6).
1977 c. 45.	Criminal Law Act 1977.	Section 11. Section 62.
1979 c. 2.	Customs and Excise Management Act 1979.	In section 138, in subsections (1) and (2), the words " or constable ".
1980 c. 43.	Magistrates' Courts Act Act 1980.	Section 49.

Sch. 7

Chapter	Short title	Extent of repeal
1980 c. 49.	Deer Act 1980.	Section 4(1)(c).
1980 c. 66.	Highways Act 1980.	Section 137(2).
1980 c. x.	County of Merseyside Act 1980.	Section 33.
1980 c. xi.	West Midlands County Council Act 1980.	Section 42.
1981 c. 14.	Public Passenger Vehicles Act 1981.	Section 25(2).
1981 c. 22.	Animal Health Act 1981.	In section 60, subsection (3), in subsection (4) the words " or apprehending ", and in subsection (5) the words " constable or ", in the second place where they occur.
1981 c. 42.	Indecent Displays (Control) Act 1981.	Section 2(1). In section 2(3), the words " within fourteen days from the date of issue of the warrant ".
1981 c. 47.	Criminal Attempts Act 1981.	Section 9(4).
1981 c. 69.	Wildlife and Countryside Act 1981.	Section 19(1)(c).
1982 c. 48.	Criminal Justice Act 1982.	Section 34.
1983 c. 2.	Representation of the People Act 1983.	In section 97(3), the words from " and " in the fifth place where it occurs to " him " in the third place where it occurs. In Schedule 1, paragraph 36.
1983 c. 20.	Mental Health Act 1983.	In section 135, in subsections (1) and (2), the words " named in the warrant ".

Part II

Enactments Repealed in Relation to Criminal Proceedings in Consequence of Part VII

Chapter	Short title	Extent of repeal
1971 c. liv.	Cornwall County Council Act 1971.	Section 98(4).
1972 c. xlvii.	Hampshire County Council Act 1972.	Section 86(2).

Part III

Enactments Repealed Generally in Consequence of Part VII

Chapter	Short title	Extent of repeal
3 & 4 Eliz. 2. c. 18.	Army Act 1955.	In section 198(1), the words " of this section and of sections 198A and 198B of this Act ". Sections 198A and 198B.
3 & 4 Eliz. 2. c. 19.	Air Force Act 1955.	In section 198(1), the words " of this section and of sections 198A and 198B of this Act ". Sections 198A and 198B.
1965 c. 20.	Criminal Evidence Act 1965.	The whole Act.
1969 c. 48.	Post Office Act 1969.	In section 93(4), the words " the Criminal Evidence Act 1965 and ". In Schedule 4, paragraph 77.
1981 c. 55.	Armed Forces Act 1981.	Section 9.
1981 c. xviii.	County of Kent Act 1981.	Section 82.
1983 c. 55.	Value Added Tax Act 1983.	In Schedule 7, paragraph 7(7) and (8).

Part IV

Enactments Repealed in Relation to Criminal Proceedings in Consequence of Part VIII

Chapter	Short title	Extent of repeal
14 & 15 Vict. c. 99.	Evidence Act 1851.	Section 13.
28 & 29 Vict. c. 18.	Criminal Procedure Act 1865.	In section 6, the words from " and a certificate " onwards.
34 & 35 Vict. c. 112.	Prevention of Crimes Act 1871.	Section 18 except the words "A previous conviction in any one part of the United Kingdom may be proved against a prisoner in any other part of the United Kingdom. ".

Sch. 7

PART V

ENACTMENTS REPEALED GENERALLY IN CONSEQUENCE OF PART VIII

Chapter	Short title	Extent of repeal
16 & 17 Vict. c. 83.	Evidence (Amendment) Act 1853.	Section 3.
46 & 47 Vict. c. 3.	Explosive Substances Act 1883.	Section 4(2).
58 & 59 Vict. c. 24.	Law of Distress Amendment Act 1895.	Section 5.
61 & 62 Vict. c. 36.	Criminal Evidence Act 1898.	In section 1, the words " and the wife or husband, as the case may be, of the person so charged ", the words (in paragraph (*b*)) " or of the wife or husband, as the case may be, of the person so charged " and paragraphs (*c*) and (*d*). Section 4. In section 6(1), the words from " notwithstanding " to the end. The Schedule.
4 & 5 Geo. 5. c. 58.	Criminal Justice Administration Act 1914.	Section 28(3).
19 & 20 Geo. 5. c. 34.	Infant Life (Preservation) Act 1929.	Section 2(5).
23 & 24 Geo. 5. c. 12.	Children and Young Persons Act 1933.	Section 15. Section 26(5).
4 & 5 Eliz. 2. c. 69.	Sexual Offences Act 1956.	Section 12(2) and (3). Section 15(4) and (5). Section 16(2) and (3). Section 39. In Schedule 3, the entry relating to section 15 of the Children and Young Persons Act 1933.
8 & 9 Eliz. 2. c. 33.	Indecency with Children Act 1960.	In section 1, subsection (2) and in subsection (3) the words " except in section 15 (which relates to the competence as a witness of the wife or husband of the accused) ".
1965 c. 72.	Matrimonial Causes Act 1965.	Section 43(1).
1968 c. 60.	Theft Act 1968.	Section 30(3).
1970 c. 55.	Family Income Supplements Act 1970.	Section 12(5).
1973 c. 38.	Social Security Act 1973.	In Schedule 23, paragraph 4.
1975 c. 14.	Social Security Act 1975.	Section 147(6).
1975 c. 16.	Industrial Injuries and Diseases (Old Cases) Act 1975.	Section 10(4).

SCH. 7

Chapter	Short title	Extent of repeal
1975 c. 61.	Child Benefit Act 1975.	Section 11(8).
1976 c. 71.	Supplementary Benefits Act 1976.	Section 26(5).
1977 c. 45.	Criminal Law Act 1977.	In section 54(3), the words " subsection (2) (competence of spouse of accused to give evidence) ".
1978 c. 37.	Protection of Children Act 1978.	Section 2(1).
1979 c. 18.	Social Security Act 1979.	Section 16.
1980 c. 43.	Magistrates' Courts Act 1980.	In Schedule 7, paragraph 4.
1982 c. 24.	Social Security and Housing Benefits Act 1982.	Section 21(6)

Part VI

Miscellaneous Repeals

Chapter	Short title	Extent of repeal
2 & 3 Vict. c. 47.	Metropolitan Police Act 1839.	Section 7.
34 & 35 Vict. c. 96.	Pedlars Act 1871.	In section 18, the words from " or " where secondly occurring to "Act," and the words from " and forthwith " to the end of the section.
1964 c. 48.	Police Act 1964.	Section 49. Section 50.
1967 c. 77.	Police (Scotland) Act 1967.	Section 5(3) and section 17(6).
1972 c. 11.	Superannuation Act 1972.	In Schedule 1, the reference to the Police Complaints Board.
1975 c. 24.	House of Commons Disqualification Act 1975.	In Part II of Schedule 1, the entry relating to the Police Complaints Board.
1975 c. 25.	Northern Ireland Assembly Disqualification Act 1975.	In Part II of Schedule 1, the entry relating to the Police Complaints Board.
1976 c. 46.	Police Act 1976.	Section 1(1) to (4). Sections 2 to 13. Section 14(2). In the Schedule, paragraphs 1 to 3, in paragraph 4, the words " remuneration " and " allowances " and paragraphs 5 to 13.